The Complete
IMMORTALIA

The Complete
IMMORTALIA

EDITED BY HAROLD H. HART

MUSICAL NOTATION BY ESTHER BOTWIN

ILLUSTRATIONS BY LINDI

Hart Publishing Company, Inc., New York City

God's plan made a hopeful beginning
But man spoiled his chances by sinning.
    We trust that the story
    Will end in God's glory—
But at present the other side's winning.

The limerick packs laughs anatomical
Into space that is quite economical.
    But the good ones I've seen
    So seldom are clean—
And the clean ones so seldom are comical.

The limerick, peculiar to English,
Is a verse form that's hard to extinguish.
    Once Congress in session
    Decreed its suppression
But people got around it by writing the last
    line without any rhyme or meter.

INTRODUCTION

IN THE PREFACE to his delicious book *Some Limericks*, Norman Douglas acknowledged that the verses in his collection might be considered obscene. "Why, so they are," he wrote, "and whoever suffers from that trying form of degeneration which is horrified at coarseness had better close this book at once."

What is considered coarse and not coarse is largely a cultural matter, and such judgments change in every age. I remember when I was a boy it was considered quite tasteless to refer to a woman as pregnant. Polite society proscribed all reference as to how the two billion people who were then on the earth happened to get there. The most that any well-mannered person was permitted to delicately say was that a woman was "in a family way." In that day, no one was supposed to mention bodily functions. Euphemisms camouflaged all trips to the bathroom. During the same era, a woman who showed as much as a naked knee at a bathing resort was considered lewd.

Today, the era of the bikini witnesses a drastically altered level of acceptable idiom. Though bluenoses may deplore, there is hardly anything that is considered sacrosanct and unmentionable. With the liberalization of our mores, it is now appropriate to publish some immortal verses which, heretofore, were reserved for stag parties.

The pieces set forth in this volume span a great many years. Some date back to at least the early 1800's; some were written yesterday. If you agree with that immortal dictum of John Keats that "a dirty mind is a joy forever," then these pieces deserve preservation.

Representing as they do the most primitive thoughts of mankind, much of the folk doggerel is fulsomely erotic. These rhymes openly express what Freud discovered everyone secretly thinks about—perhaps in this day and age, no longer so secretly.

Few of the verses as they are presented here have appeared in public print; some have been surreptitiously preserved in the august archives of libraries open only to scholars; some have been privately reprinted from time to time. A handful, miserably bowdlerized, were sufficiently emasculated to pass the censors of what one now hopes is a bygone era. Some make their very first appearance in this volume. This is certainly true of a number of original pieces.

Since some of these verses were nothing more than street doggerel, some of the lines were out of rhythm and, in some cases, out of rhyme. The editor has attempted to patch these up for better effect. Similarly, liberties have been taken in substituting current expression for archaic idiom which would be difficult to comprehend.

The great majority of these pieces are of unknown origin. The naive quality of some verses makes it clear that they sprang from unlettered sources and were passed along by word of mouth. However, it is readily apparent that not all the pieces were spawned in the marketplace. Some of the verse and undoubtedly most of the parodies were penned by sophisticated rhymsters.

The limerick is now an abiding part of our literature. A highly disciplined verse form, compact and clever, it tells a story in only five lines. Unlike most basic forms of English verse such as the sonnet and the triolet, the limerick was not borrowed from other countries but is indigenously English, perhaps the only form in poetry that can be claimed to be an original English creation.

Undoubtedly, the limerick is the most quoted of all verse forms extant today. From the drawing room to the classroom, whether recited in a surreptitious whisper or blared forth uproariously, the limerick has captivated almost every echelon of society. Popular everywhere, it has especially become the darling of the intellectual.

The limerick reflects the temper of its day. Additions to this great fund of versification have been made by outstanding poets and publicists. Some of the most widely recited limericks have been ascribed, perhaps apocryphally, to Alfred Lord Tennyson, Norman Douglas, Eugene Field, Don Marquis, Heywood Broun, Woodrow Wilson, among others.

Back in the 1860's, Edward Lear penned these rhythmical five-line ditties for children. But the form soon bounded out of the nursery onto the campus; and from there into the marketplace, the counting house, and the army. Once out on the streets and in full contact with the foibles and fantasies of the common folk, the limerick began to reflect everyday thoughts more plain-spokenly. The more pungent, punchy, and bawdy, the more easily were these verses memorized, and the more frequently were they quoted.

The subjects treated by the anonymous authors of these stanzas run the entire gamut of sexual activity. Fantasy has no limits, and many of these verses rise to heights of superlative exaggeration.

The songs set forth in these pages include sea shanties, barrack room ballads, night club favorites, college songs, and American, English, and Scottish folk verse of several eras. Though most of the melodies are old, many of the verses appear here for the first time.

For the most part, these stanzas are forthrightly bawdy; much of the charm of these pieces derives from bald assertion. There is little attempt at euphemism. The editor has taken certain liberties with the material. Verses of Scottish origin, for example, have been translated into modern English idiom. Lines of uneven meter have been rendered more rhymical. Unrhymed couplets have been amended.

The musical notation has deliberately been kept to a primer level. There are no indications in Italian nomenclature of mood or pace. As the Romans used to say, *res ipsa loquitur*—"the thing speaks for itself." It is unlikely that anyone would be so crass as to drone through *The Bastard King of England,* or that anyone would be so insensitive as to race through *That Little Ball of Yarn.* The experienced guitar player will easily sense the mood of each song without stage direction. He will rollick with *Aboard the Good Ship Venus,* and roar out *Don't Call Me,* and solemnly intone *The Shit-*

house Rag. Hopefully, each singer's rendition will accord proper homage to these classics.

The contents of this volume are rounded out with a potpourri of puns, graffiti, riddles, etc.—that kind of catch thing that will be said one day in New York, and then travel, as if by wireless telegraph, to be heard the next day in San Francisco. Of the thousands of tidbits of this type created unendingly, only a few are particularly clever, stand the test of time, and deserve to be immortalized in print. This volume contains, it is hoped, the very best of this genre. Undoubtedly, some of the choicest morsels have eluded us.

Finally, I want to say that this volume is meant to arouse—not the prurient interest—only one's risibilities.

HAROLD H. HART

CONTENTS

The Complete
IMMORTALIA

Riddles

What's the difference between a bad marksman and a
   constipated owl?

   A bad marksman shoots and shoots and never hits.

✳   ✳   ✳

What's the difference between a rooster and a shyster?
   A rooster clucks defiance.

✳   ✳   ✳

What's the difference between a eunuch and an Eskimo?
   *A eunuch is a massive vassal with a passive tassel, while
   an Eskimo is a rigid midget with a frigid digit.*

✳   ✳   ✳

What do they call an abortion in Prague?
   A cancelled Czech.

✳   ✳   ✳

Why is a passionate kiss like a spider?
   Both lead to the undoing of the fly.

What is it that two men can do with ease, a woman and a
man can do with difficulty, and two women can't do
at all?

Piss in the same pot.

❋   ❋   ❋

What's the difference between a vitamin and a hormone?

You can't hear a vitamin.

❋   ❋   ❋

Who were the three most constipated men in the Bible?

The first was Cain—he wasn't able.
The second was Moses—he took two tablets.
The third was Balaam—he had trouble with his ass.

❋   ❋   ❋

What do you call an uncircumised Jewish baby?

A girl.

What's the difference between a seagull and a baby?

A seagull flits along the shore.

❊   ❊   ❊

What has four legs and flies?

Two pairs of pants.

❊   ❊   ❊

What's the difference between a miniature circus and a
Broadway chorus line?

A circus is an array of cunning stunts.

❊   ❊   ❊

Why does a cow have a long face?

*If you had your tits pulled twice a day, and were fucked
only once a year, wouldn't you have a long face, too?*

❊   ❊   ❊

What are the three most insulting words in the world?

Is it in?

What's more profitable: a one-story whorehouse or a two-story whorehouse?

A one-story whorehouse 'cause there's no fuckin' overhead.

* * *

What's indecent?

When it's in long, and it's in hard, and it's in deep, then it's in decent.

* * *

What is better than honor?
In 'er!

* * *

What's the difference between a sweater girl and a sewing machine?

A sewing machine has only one bobbin.

What's the difference between an opera director and a baby?

A baby sucks his fingers.

※   ※   ※

Who was the greatest golfer in the Bible?

King Solomon—he shot a thousand holes with two balls.

※   ※   ※

Why is love like toilet paper?

After you tear off the first piece, the rest comes easy.

※   ※   ※

Who's the bravest man in the world?

The peanut vendor—he whistles while his nuts are burning.

※   ※   ※

What's the difference between a sin and a shame?

It's a sin to put it in; it's a shame to take it out.

What's the difference between frustration and utter
  frustration?

*Frustration is the first time you find out that you can't
do it the second time. Utter frustration is the second
time you find out that you can't do it the first time.*

❊   ❊   ❊

How do porcupines make love?

Very carefully.

❊   ❊   ❊

What's the difference between a well-stacked blonde and
  the same dame in the nighttime?

In the daytime she's fair and buxom.

❊   ❊   ❊

What's the difference between a skinny dame and a
  counterfeit dollar bill?

A counterfeit dollar bill is a phony buck.

Limericks

There was a young maid from Madras

Who had a magnificent ass;

    Not rounded and pink,

    As you probably think—

It was grey, had long ears, and ate grass.

There was a young sailor named Bates

Who danced the fandango on skates.

    But a fall on his cutlass

    Has rendered him nutless,

And practically useless on dates.

To his bride said the lynx-eyed detective,

"Can it be that my eyesight's defective?

    Has your east tit the least bit

    The best of the west tit?

Or is it a trick of perspective?"

A mathematician named Hall

Has a hexahedronical ball,

    And the cube of its weight

    Times his pecker, plus eight,

Is his phone number—give him a call.

There was a young girl named Ann Heuser

Who swore that no man could surprise her.

But Pabst took a chance,

Found a Schlitz in her pants,

And now she is sadder Budweiser.

There was an old Count of Swoboda

Who would not pay a whore what he owed her.

So with great *savoir-faire*

She stood on a chair,

And pissed in his whiskey-and-soda.

There was a young fellow named Bart
Who strained every shit through a fart.
Each tip-tapered turd
Was the very last word
In this deft and most intricate art.

On a maiden a man once begat
Cute triplets named Nat, Tat, and Pat;
'Twas fun in the breeding
But hell in the feeding:
She hadn't a spare tit for Tat.

There was a young tar from the sea

Who screwed a baboon in a tree.

    The results were most horrid—

    All ass and no forehead,

Four balls and a purple goatee.

There was a young lady named White

Found herself in a terrible plight:

    A mucker named Tucker

    Had struck her, the fucker,

The bugger, the bastard, the shite!

There was a young fellow of Kent

Who had a peculiar bent.

> He collected the turds
>
> Of various birds,

And ate them for lunch during Lent.

There once was a harlot at Yale

With her price-list tattooed on her tail,

> And on her behind,
>
> For the sake of the blind,

She had it embroidered in Braille.

There was an old lady of Cheadle

Who sat down in church on a needle.

The needle, though blunt,

Penetrated her cunt,

But was promptly removed by the beadle.

There was a young man from Sioux Falls

Renowned in vaudeville halls;

His favorite trick

Was to stand on his prick

And then slide off the stage on his balls!

Sobbed the wife of a worrisome vcep,

"I'm so tired and worn I could weep.

    It's my husband's demand

    For a tit in each hand—

And the bastard walks 'round in his sleep!"

An impish young fellow named James

Had a passion for idiot games.

    He lighted the hair

    Of his lady's affair

And laughed as she peed through the flames.

THE ACROBAT

There was a young fellow named Dick
Who perfected a wonderful trick:

> He'd get an erection,

> And scorn all protection,

Then balance himself on his prick.

'Twas a fearful and wonderful sight;
And the ladies all shrieked with delight;

> But the men were less zealous,

> For it made them all jealous,

And they said Dick had no copyright!

Then each of them tried it and failed,

While their wives looked on helpless and wailed

    For each one would teeter

    And fall on his peter,

Or managed to get all derailed.

So Dick was the toast of the town;

There was nothing too good for that clown,

    And the wives all came flocking

    To the acrobat's cocking,

While the husbands deplored his renown.

The Acrobat

And then came the best part of all:

That number would bring down the hall;

    For his tour-de-force trick

    Was to straddle his prick,

And wheel out of sight on one ball!

  The ladies all ran to tease Dick

That the Frenchman had bettered his trick;

    So he straddled and struggled,

    And one ball he juggled,

But he knocked out his prop with a kick.

The Acrobat

Now the tragedy didn't end there;

For as Richard whirled down through the air,

    His prick became tied

    In a knot that defied

All attempts to untangle its snare.

Most men would have died of remorse;

But Dick found another resource:

    For pretzels he'd pose

    With his twisted up hose,

And he made a nice income, of course.

A lady while dining at Crewe

Found an elephant's whang in her stew.

Said the waiter, "Don't shout,

Or wave it about,

Or the rest will be wanting one, too."

There was a young girl of Baroda

Who built an erotic pagoda;

The walls of its halls

Were festooned with the balls

And the tools of the fools who bestrode her.

There was a young blade of Connaught

Whose prick was remarkably short.

When he got into bed

His lady friend said,

"This isn't a prick, it's a wart."

There was a young fellow of Buckingham,

Wrote a treatise on cunts and on fucking 'em;

But later this work

Was eclipsed by a Turk

Wrote an opus on ass-holes and sucking 'em.

I once knew a clever young bitch

Who owned a self-frigger the which

    She would use with delight

    Far into the night,

Twenty bucks—Abercrombie & Fitch.

There once was a young man from Greenwich

Whose balls were all covered with spinach;

    So long was his tool

    It was wound on a spool

In-ich, by in-ich, by in-ich!

"It's no good," said Lady Maud Hoare,

"I can't concentrate any more.

I'm all in a sweat

And the sheets are quite wet,

And look at the time—half past four!"

Said the mythical King of Algiers

To his harem assembled, "My dears,

You may think it odd of me

But I'm tired of sodomy;

Tonight there'll be fucking!" (*Loud cheers!*)

There was a young farmer of Nant,

Whose conduct was gay and gallant;

For he fucked all his dozens

Of nieces and cousins,

In addition, of course, to his aunt.

From the depths of the crypt at St. Giles

Came a scream that resounded for miles.

Said the vicar, "Good gracious!

Has Father Ignatius

Forgotten the Bishop has piles?"

There was a young lady of Twickenham

Who used to take cocks without pickin' 'em.

    She'd kneel on the sod,

    And pray to her God

To lengthen and strengthen and thicken 'em.

Nymphomaniacal Alice

Used a dynamite stick for a phallus;

    They found her vagina

    In North Carolina

And half of her ass-hole in Dallas.

A bather whose clothing was strewed

By breezes that left her quite nude

Saw a man come along,

And, unless I am wrong,

You expected this line to be lewd.

There was a young lady named Clair

Who possessed a magnificent pair;

Or that's what I thought

'Til I saw one get caught

On a thorn, and begin to lose air.

There was a young fellow from Florida

Who liked a friend's wife, so he borrowed her.

    When they got into bed

    He cried, "God strike me dead!

Now this ain't a cunt—it's a corridor!"

In Wall Street a girl named Irene

Made an offering somewhat obscene:

    She stripped herself bare

    And offered a share

To Merrill Lynch, Fenner and Beane.

THE BISHOP OF BIRMINGHAM

There were two young ladies of Birmingham,

And this is the story concerning 'em:

    They lifted the frock

    And diddled the cock

Of the Bishop as he was confirming 'em.

The Bishop was nobody's fool—

He'd been to a large public school;

    He took down his britches

    And diddled those bitches

With his ten-inch Episcopal tool.

But that didn't bother those two;

They said as the Bishop withdrew:

    "Oh, the Vicar is quicker

    And thicker and slicker

And longer and stronger than you."

I once knew a very queer lass

Who had a triangular ass.

  Now it might sound absurd

  But the shape of her turd

Was a stately pyramidal mass!

A thrifty old man named McEwen

Inquired, "Why bother with screwing?

  It's safer and cleaner

  To finger your wiener,

And besides you can see what you're doing."

There was a young lady of Worcester

Who complained that many men goosed her.

    So over her caper

    She laid some sandpaper

Now they goose her much less than they used ter.

A habit obscene and unsavory

Holds the Bishop of Wessex in slavery.

    With maniacal howls

    He deflowers young owls

Which he keeps in an underground aviary.

There was a young fellow named Wyatt

Who kept a big girl on the quiet;

But down on the wharf

He maintained a dwarf,

In case he should go on a diet.

There was a young Turkish cadet—

And this is the damnedest one yet—

His tool was so long

And incredibly strong

He could bugger six Greeks *en brochette*.

There was a young fellow named Kimble

Whose prick was exceedingly nimble

But so fragile, so slender

So dainty and tender

He kept it encased in a thimble.

There was a plug-ugly named Ug

Who plugged his cock into a jug.

Wrapped the jug in a rug,

Gave the whole thing a tug,

And developed one helluva fug!

There was a young man of Cape Horn

Who wished he had never been born;

    And he wouldn't have been

    If his father had seen

That the end of the rubber was torn.

There was a young fellow from Leeds

Rashly swallowed a package of seeds.

    Great tufts of fine grass

    Sprouted out of his ass

And his balls were all covered with weeds.

There once was a Bishop of Treet

Who decided to be indiscreet,

But after one round

To his horror he found

You repeat, and repeat, and repeat!

There was a young girl from France

Who jumped on a bus in a trance.

Six passengers fucked her,

Besides the conductor,

And the driver shot twice in his pants.

A nympho by name of Calpurnia

Grew hot and hotter and burnier.

    So she fucked and she fucked

    And she fucked and she fucked

'Til she fucked herself into a hernia.

A steward who worked on a clipper

Was quite a bit of a nipper;

    He plugged up his ass

    With fragments of glass

And circumcised the skipper.

There was a young man of Devizes

Whose balls were of two different sizes.

The one was so small

'Twas nothing at all—

But the other—it won several prizes!

A pretty young harlot of Crete

Used to hawk her meat in the street.

Ambling out one fine day

In a most casual way,

She clapped up the whole British fleet.

There was a young fellow named Price

Who dabbled in all sorts of vice:

He had virgins and boys

And mechanical toys—

And on Mondays, he meddled with mice!

There was a smart miss had a hernia

Who said to her doctor, "Goldernia,

When improving my middle

Be sure you don't fiddle

With matters that do not concernia."

There was a young man from Brighton

Who thought he'd at last found a tight 'un.

    He said, "O my love,

    It fits like a glove."

Said she, "But you're not in the right 'un."

There was a young fellow of Warwick

Who had reason for feeling euphoric;

    For he could by election

    Have triune erection:

Ionic, Corinthian, Doric.

There was a young man from Berlin

Whose tool was the size of a pin.

    Said his girl with a laugh

    As she fondled that shaft,

"Well, *this* won't be much of a sin."

A flatulent Roman named Titus

Was taken with sudden colitis;

    And the venerable Forum

    Lost most of its quorum

As he farted up half of the situs.

There was a young man of Khartoum

Who lured a poor girl to her doom.

    He not only fucked her,

       And buggered and sucked her—

But left her to pay for the room.

There was a young lady of Ealing,

Endowed with such delicate feeling,

    When she read on the door:

    "Don't piss on the floor"—

She lay down and pissed on the ceiling.

There was a young girl of East Anglia

Whose loins were a tangle of ganglia.

Her mind was a webbing

Of Freud and Krafft-Ebing

And all sorts of other new-fanglia.

There was a young fellow named Cass

Whose balls were made of spun glass.

He'd clink them together

And play *Stormy Weather*,

While lightning shot out of his ass.

A widow whose singular vice

Was to keep her late husband on ice,

    Said, "It's been hard since I lost him—

    I'll never defrost him!

Cold comfort, but cheap at the price."

A brainy professor named Zed

Dreamed one night of a buxom co-ed;

    He mussed her and bussed her

    And otherwise fussed her,

But the action was all in his head.

There was an old man of Tagore

Who tried out his cook on the floor;

    He used Bridget's twidget

    To fidget his digit,

And now she won't cook any more.

There was a young woman of Croft

Who played with herself in a loft,

    Having reasoned that candles

    Could never cause scandals,

Besides which they never went soft.

THE MAN WHO ONLY SCREWED

There was a young fellow named Fyfe

Whose marriage was ruined for life,

    For he had an aversion

    To every perversion

And only liked screwing his wife.

Well, one year the poor woman struck

And she wept, and she cursed at her luck,

    "Oh, where has it gotten us

    This goddamn monotonous

Fuck after fuck after fuck?"

There was a young lady at sea

Who complained that it hurt her to pee.

"Aha!" said the mate,

"That accounts for the state

Of the cook and the captain and me."

Did you hear about young Henry Lockett?

He was blown down the street by a rocket.

The force of the blast

Blew his balls up his ass,

And his pecker was found in his pocket.

A pretty young boy known as Kevin

Was raped in a pasture by seven

    Lascivious beasts—

    Oh, those Anglican priests!—

For of such is the kingdom of heaven.

King Louis gave a lesson in "Class,"

Simultaneously sexing a lass.

    When she used the word "Damn"

    He rebuked her: "Please ma'am,

Keep a more civil tongue up my ass."

Well screwed was a boy named Delpasse

By all of the lads in his class.

But he said, with a yawn,

"Now the novelty's gone

And it's only a pain in the ass."

A pansy by name of Ben Bloom

Took a lesbian up to his room,

They talked the whole night

As to who had the right

To do what, with which, and to whom.

A mortician who practiced in Fyfe,

Made love to the corpse of his wife.

"I couldn't know, Judge.

She was cold, didn't budge—

Just the same as she acted in life."

I dined with the Duchess of Lee

Who asked, "Do you fart when you pee?"

Replied I, with quick wit,

"Do you belch when you shit?

Say, Duchess, chalk one up for me."

There once was a girl named McGoffin

Who was diddled amazingly often.

    At sex, never bested,

    She never was rested

Until she was screwed in her coffin.

A reckless young man from Fort Blaney

Made love to a spinster named Janie.

    When his friends said, "Oh dear,

    She's so old and so queer."

He replied, "But the day was *so* rainy!"

A fencing instructor named Fisk

In sex was terribly brisk.

    So fast was his action

    The Fitzgerald contraction

Foreshortened his foil to a disk.

A Bishop whose see was Vermont

Used to jerk himself off in the font.

    The baptistry stank

    With an odor most rank,

And no one would sit up in front.

There was a young monk of Dundee

Who complained that it hurt him to pee.

He said, "Pax vobiscum!

Now why won't the piss come?

I'm afraid I've the C-L-A-P."

A charming young lady from Brussels

Takes pride in her vaginal muscles.

For any erection

Her timing's perfection

And she never hurries—she hustles.

A lovesick skydiver named Sherm

Bailed out with his prick long and firm;

    Two jerks plus a spasm

    Produced an orgasm,

And he spelled out "I love you" in sperm.

A freshman with visions Elysian

Once screwed an appendix incision,

    But the girl of his choice

    Could hardly rejoice

At this horrible lack of precision.

A notorious harlot named Hearst

In the pleasures of men is well-versed.

Reads a sign o'er the head

Of her well-rumpled bed:

"The Customer Always Comes First!"

A trucker by name of McBride

Had a young whore that he hired

To fuck when not trucking.

But trucking *plus* fucking

Got him so fucking tired he got fired.

There once was a warden of Wadham

Who approved of the folkways of Sodom,

    "For a man might," he said

    "Have a very poor head

But be a fine fellow, at bottom."

There was a young lady from Brent—

When her husband's pecker it bent,

    She said with a sigh,

    "Oh, why must it die?

Let's fill it with Portland Cement."

There was a young lady named Hilda

Who went driving one night with a builda.

   He said that he should

   That he could and he would,

And he did and it pretty near killda.

There was a young man from Australia

Who painted his ass like a dahlia.

   The colors were fine;

   The drawing—divine!

But the smell was a terrible failure!

There was a young Catholic named Alice,

Who peed in the Bishop's new chalice;

    But that worthy agreed

    That 'twas done out of need,

And not out of Protestant malice.

There was a young girl from Madrid.

Who learned she was having a kid.

    By holding her water

    Two months and a quarter,

She drowned the poor bastard, she did.

A maiden who lived in Virginny

Had a cunt that could bark, neigh, and whinny.

    The hunting set chased her;

    But soon they displaced her

When the pitch of her organ went tinny.

There was a young man of St. Johns

Who wanted to bugger the swans.

    "Oh no," said the porter,

    "Go bugger my daughter—

Them swans is reserved for the Dons."

There was a young man of Belgravia,

Who cared not for God nor for Savior;

    He walked down the Strand

    With his prick in his hand,

And was had for indecent behavior.

There was a soprano from Reggio,

Whose cunt was trained in solfeggio;

    One day a contraction

    Caused such a reaction,

She pissed—and missed an arpeggio!

There was a young lady named Hitchin

Who was scratching her crotch in the kitchen.

Her mother said, "Rose,

It's the crabs, I suppose."

Said Rose, "And the buggers are itchin'!"

I have been on dozens of larks;

I like it indoors, not in parks.

You feel more at ease;

Your ass doesn't freeze;

And strollers don't make snide remarks.

A disgusting young man named McGill

Made his neighbors exceedingly ill,

   When they learned of his habits

   Involving white rabbits

And a bird with a flexible bill.

At the orgy I fucked twenty-two;

And, man, was I glad to get through.

   A whole night of sexing

   Turns boring and vexing—

But at orgies, what else can you do?

A broken-down lecher named Tupps

Was heard to confess in his cups:

"The height of my folly

Was diddling a collie—

But I got a nice price for the pups."

There was a young man from St. Paul

Whose cock was exceedingly small.

Now it might do for a keyhole

Or a little girl's pechole

But for a big girl like me—not at all!

'Tis reported that Prince Montezuma

Once had an affair with a puma.

  The puma in play

  Clawed both balls away:

An example of animal humor.

A prosperous merchant of Rhone

Took orders for cunt on the phone;

  Or the same could be baled,

  Stamped, labeled, and mailed

To a limited parcel-post zone.

There was a young fellow named Sweeney

Whose girl was a terrible meanie.

The hatch of her snatch

Had a catch that would latch—

She could only be screwed by Houdini.

There was a young girl of Cape Cod

Who thought babes were fashioned by God,

But 'twas not the Almighty

Who hiked up her nightie—

'Twas Roger, the lodger, by God!

There was a young fellow from Boston

Who rode around in an Austin.

There was room for his ass

And a gallon of gas,

But his balls hung outside, and he lost 'em.

A dentist, young Doctor Malone,

Got a charming girl patient alone;

And in his depravity,

He filled the wrong cavity—

And my how his practice has grown!

An agreeable girl named Miss Doves

Likes to jack off the young men she loves.

    She will use her bare fist

    If the fellows insist

But she really prefers to wear gloves.

There was a young lady of Rheims,

Who amazingly pissed in four streams.

    A friend poked around

    And a coat button found

Wedged tightly in one of her seams.

An Argentine gaucho named Bruno

Once said, "There is one thing I do know:

A woman is fine

And a sheep is divine—

But a llama's Numero Uno!"

A farmer I know named O'Doole

Has a long and incredible tool.

He can use it to plow,

Or to diddle a cow,

Or just as a cue-stick at pool.

There once was a gangster named Brown,
The wiliest bastard in town.
    He was caught by the G-men
    Shooting his semen
Where the cops would all slip and fall down.

There once was a young man of Kent
Whose tool was so long that it bent.
    To save himself trouble
    He put it in double—
And instead of coming, he went!

There was an old man of Madrid

Who went to an auction to bid.

    In the first lot they sold

    Was an ancient commode—

And, my god, when they lifted the lid!

There was a young lady from Spain

Whose face was exceedingly plain,

    But her cunt had a pucker

    That made the men fuck her,

Again, and again, and again.

There was a young man named Dave,

Who kept a dead whore in a cave.

    Said he, "I admit

    She does smell a bit,

But look at the money I save!"

There's an over-sexed lady named Whyte

Who insists on a dozen a night.

    A fellow named Cheddar

    Had the brashness to wed her—

And his chance of survival is slight.

There once was a lady from Arden

Who sucked off a man in a garden.

    He said, "My dear Flo,

    Where does all that stuff go?"

And she said, "*(swallow hard)*—I beg pardon?"

There was a young lady of Chichester

Who made all the saints in their niches stir.

    One morning, at matins,

    Her breasts in white satins

Made the Bishop of Chichester's britches stir.

A big Catholic layman named Fox

Makes his living by sucking off cocks.

In spells of depression

He goes to confession,

And jacks off the priest in his box.

There was a young fellow named Lancelot

Whom his neighbors all looked on askance a lot.

Whenever he'd pass

A presentable lass,

The front of his pants would advance a lot.

There was a young girl of Aberystwyth

Who took grain to the mill to get grist with.

The miller's son, Jack,

Laid her flat on her back

And united the organs they pissed with.

There once was a young man from Greenwich

Whose balls were all covered with spinach;

So long was his tool

It was wound on a spool

In-ich, by in-ich, by in-ich!

There was a young harlot from Kew

Who filled her vagina with glue.

She said with a grin,

"If they pay to get in,

They'll pay to get out of it, too."

There was a young fellow named Bliss

Whose sex life was strangely amiss,

For even with Venus

His recalcitrant penis

Would seldom do better than t
                                   h
                                   i
                                   s.

There was a young girl from Detroit

Who at fucking was very adroit;

    She'd contract her vagina

    To a pin-point or finer

Or widen it out like a quoit.

There was a young man of Bengal

Who swore he had only one ball,

    But two sons-of-bitches

    Pulled off his britches,

And the bastard had no balls at all.

THAT FELLOW NAMED SKINNER

There was a young fellow named Skinner

Who took a young lady to dinner.

    They started to dine

    At a quarter past nine—

And at twenty to ten it was in 'er.

    The dinner? No, Skinner.

    Skinner was in 'er *before* dinner.

There was a young fellow named Tupper

Who took a young lady to supper.

They sat down to dine,

At a quarter to nine,

And at twenty to ten it was up 'er.

Not the supper—not Tupper—it was some

son-of-a-bitch named Skinner!

There was a young girl of Llewellyn
Whose breasts were as big as a melon.
They were big, it is true,
But her cunt was big too,
Like a bifocal, full-color, aerial view
of Cape Horn and the Straits of Magellan.

There was a young man from Racine
Who invented a fucking machine:
Both concave and convex,
It would fit either sex—
And so perfectly simple to clean!

There was a young plumber named Lee,

Who plumbed his girl down by the sea;

Said the lady, "Stop plumbing!

I hear someone coming."

Said the plumber, still plumbing, "That's me."

A newlywed couple from Goshen

Spent their honeymoon sailing the ocean.

In twenty-eight days

They screwed eighty ways—

Imagine such fucking devotion!

There was a young man named Hughes

Who swore off all kinds of booze.

    He said, "When I'm muddled

    My senses get fuddled,

And I pass up too many screws."

There once was a monk of Camyre

Who was seized with a carnal desire.

    And the primary cause

    Was the abbess' drawers

Which were hung up to dry by the fire.

A lecherous Bishop of Peoria,

In a state of constant euphoria,

Enjoyed having fun

With a whore or a nun

While chanting the *Sanctus* and *Gloria*.

There was a young man named Mirkin

Who kept on a-jerkin' his gherkin;

Said his wife to Mirkin,

"Your duty you're shirkin'

That gherkin's for firkin', not jerkin'."

There once was a lovely young miss

Who went down to the river to read.

A young man in a punt

Stuck an oar in her eye

And now she has to wear glasses!

In the Garden of Eden lay Adam

Complacently stroking his madam,

And loud was his mirth

For he knew that on earth

There were only two balls—and he had 'em.

There was a young girl from Sofia

Who succumbed to her lover's desire.

　　She said, "It's a sin,

　　But now that it's in,

Could you shove it a few inches higher?"

There once was a girl of Siam

Who said to her love, young Kiam,

　　"If you take me, of course,

　　You must do it by force,

But God knows you are stronger than I am."

A lady on climbing Mount Shasta

Complained as the mountain grew vaster,

   That it wasn't the climb

   Nor the dirt nor the grime

But the ice on her ass that harassed her.

There was a young man from St. Paul's

Who read *Harper's Bazaar* and *McCall's*

   'Til he grew such a passion

   For feminine fashion

That he knitted a snood for his balls.

A comely young widow named Ransom
Was ravished three times in a hansom.
　　When she cried out for more
　　A voice from the floor
Said, "Lady, I'm Simpson, not Samson."

A corpulent lady named Kroll
Had an idea exceedingly droll:
　　She went to a ball
　　Dressed in nothing at all
And backed in as a Parker House roll.

THE FARTER FROM SPARTA

There was a young fellow from Sparta,
A really magnificent farter,
On the strength of one bean
He'd fart *God Save the Queen*,
And Beethoven's *Moonlight Sonata*.

He could vary, with proper persuasion,
His fart to suit any occasion.
He could fart like a flute,
Like a lark, like a lute,
This highly fartistic Caucasian.

He'd fart a gavotte for a starter,

And fizzle a fine serenata.

　He could play on his anus

　The Coriolanus:

Oof, boom, er-tum, tootle, hum tah-dah!

He was great in the *Christmas Cantata,*

He could double-stop fart *The Toccata,*

　He'd boom from his ass

　Bach's B-Minor Mass,

And in counterpoint, *La Traviata.*

Spurred on by a very high wager

With an envious Lieutenant Major,

He proceeded to fart

The complete oboe part

Of the Haydn *Octet in B-major*.

It went off in capital style,

And he farted it through with a smile;

Then, feeling quite jolly,

He tried the finale,

Blowing double-stopped farts all the while.

The selection was tough, I admit,

But it did not dismay him one bit,

'Til with ass thrown aloft

He suddenly coughed—

And collapsed in a shower of shit!

A painter of pop art named Jacques

Painted each canvas to shock.

    Outsized genitalia

    Gave the viewers heart failure

But the critics just sneered, "Poppycock!"

There was a young fellow named Gluck

Who found himself shit out of luck.

    Though he petted and wooed,

    When he tried to get screwed

He found virgins don't give a fuck.

There was a young fellow named Hyde

Who fell down a privy and died.

His unfortunate brother

Then fell down another

And now they're interred side by side.

There was a young lady of Dexter

Whose husband exceedingly vexed her,

For whenever they'd start

He'd unfailingly fart

With a blast that damn nearly unsexed her.

There was a young lady of France

Who went to the palace to dance.

She danced with a Turk

Till he got in his dirk,

And now she can't button her pants.

I sat next to the Duchess at tea;

It was just as I feared it would be:

Her rumblings abdominal

Were truly phenomenal,

And everyone thought it was me!

There was a young fellow named Charteris
Put his hand where his young lady's garter is.
She said, "I don't mind,
Up higher you'll find
The place where my pisser and farter is."

There was a young lawyer named Rex
Who was sadly deficient in sex.
Arraigned for exposure
He said with composure,
"De minimis non curat lex." *

* The law is not concerned with trifles.

There was a young lady of Wantage

Of whom the Town Clerk took advantage.

    Said the County Surveyor,

    "Of course you must pay her:

You've altered the line of her frontage."

A young violinist in Rio

Was seducing a lady named Cleo.

    As she took down her panties,

    She said, "No *andantes;*

I want this *allegro con brio!*"

There was a young girl from Lancaster

Who'd do anything anyone asked her.

   But when she got spliced

   She got so high priced

Only Jesus H. Christ and John Jacob Astor.

A weary old lecher named Blott

Took a luscious young blonde on his yacht.

   Too lazy to rape her,

   He made darts out of paper,

Which he leisurely tossed at her twat.

A pathetic old maid of Bordeaux

Fell in love with a dashing young beau.

To entice his regard

She would squat in his yard

And appealingly piss in the snow.

T here was a young couple named Kelly

Who were forced to walk belly to belly,

Because in their haste

They used library paste

Which they thought was vaginal jelly.

There was a young man of Kildare

Who was fucking a girl on the stair.

    The bannister broke,

    But he doubled his stroke

And finished her off in mid-air.

A young curate, just new to the cloth,

At sex was surely no sloth.

    He preached masturbation

    To his whole congregation,

And was washed down the aisle on the froth.

A gentle old lady I knew
Was dozing one day in her pew;
When the preacher yelled "Sin!"
She said, "Count me in!
—And as soon as the service is through!"

A progressive professor named Tinners
Held classes each evening for sinners.
They were graded and spaced
So the very debased
Would not be held back by beginners.

There was a young lady named Hall,

Wore a newspaper dress to a ball.

The dress caught on fire

And burned her entire

Front page, sporting section, and all.

There was a young man from New Haven

Who had an affair with a raven.

He said with a grin

As he wiped off his chin,

"Nevermore!"

There was a young lady of Norway

Who hung by her toes in a doorway.

    She said to her beau:

    "Just look at me, Joe,

I think I've discovered one more way."

There was a young lady named Duff

With a lovely, luxuriant muff.

    In his haste to get in her

    One eager beginner

Lost both of his balls in the rough.

An old archeologist, Throstle,

Discovered a marvelous fossil.

    He knew from its bend

    And the knob on the end

'Twas the peter of Paul the Apostle.

There was a young lady in Reno

Who lost all her dough playing keeno.

    But she lay on her back

    And opened her crack—

And now she owns the casino.

LEXICON

alimony   The fucking you get for the fucking you got.

brassiere   A device that makes mountains out of molehills.

chutzpah   A guy taking a crap on someone's doorstep and
then ringing the bell and asking for toilet paper.

height of presumption   A falsie manufacturer advertising,
"Beware of imitations."

home cooking   Where many a man thinks his wife is.

kept woman   A lady who wears mink by day and fox by night.

lady   A woman who never smokes or drinks and only
swears when it slips out.

marriage   An occupation which pays the highest wages for
unskilled labor.

minute man   A guy who double-parks in front of a
whorehouse.

mother's day   Nine months after father's day.

perfect secretary   One who never misses a period.

quickie   No sooner spread than done.

rectal specialist   Super duper pooper snooper.

rugby   A game played by men with peculiarly shaped balls.

secretary   A device you screw on a desk and it takes dictation.

sob sister   A girl who sits on your knees and bawls and makes it hard for you.

height of propriety   A guy letting a fart in a public toilet and then turning around to everybody and saying, "Excuse me."

vice squad   A pussy posse.

welsh rarebit   A Cardiff virgin.

wild goose   One that is an inch off center.

Folk Rhymes

The Daring Fly

The little fly flew through the door,
He flew into the grocery store;
He shit on the cheese, and shit on the ham,
Then he wiped his feet on the grocery man.

When the grocery man saw what he'd done,
He went and got his Gatling gun;
Then he chased that fly all over the place,
And tried to shoot him in the face.

But that little fly was awfully slick;
He showed that grocery man a trick:
He flew around the store, and then
Went over and shit on the ham again.

And when he'd finished his dirty work,
He went over and lit on the lady clerk;
He climbed her leg 'way past her knee,
And tickled her into ecstasy.

He fluttered so fast he made her sigh,
And she softly murmured, "Oh my! Oh my!"
Then she closed her legs and held her breath,
And the poor little fly was smothered to death.

Retort

She lay stark nude between the sheets,
    So nice and fat and chubby;
And I myself beside her lay,
    My hand upon her bubby.

I kissed her lips in crazy glee;
    Her ass had great allure.
Our thighs did intermingle,
    And I began to screw 'er.

"Pull out!" she cried, "Pull out! Pull out!
    Or I'll get into trouble."
I did, and on her snow-white breast
    A stream did squirt and bubble.

I looked upon the gluey flow,
    And with a wisecrack burst—
"You know, that is the youngest child
    That you have ever nursed."

She scooped the goo with one fair hand,
    And with a scornful "Ha!"
She threw the load into my face
    And said, *"Go kiss your Pa!"*

Christmas in the Workhouse

It was Christmas in the workhouse,
    The best day of the year;
And the paupers all were happy
    For their guts were full of beer.

The warden of the workhouse
    Strode through those dismal halls,
And wished 'em, "Merry Christmas,"
    And the paupers answered, "Balls!"

This made the warden angry,
    And he swore by all the Gods,
They'd have no Christmas puddin'——
    The lousy lot of sods.

Up sprang a war-scarred vet'ran
    Who had stormed the Khyber Pass,
"We don't want your Christmas puddin',
    Shove it up your fuckin' ass!"

The Corkscrew Thread

There was a young fellow named Dead-eye Dick,
Who was cursed from birth with a corkscrew prick.
His life was spent in an aimless hunt
To find a girl with a corkscrew cunt.
But when he found her, the guy dropped dead—
For the goddam thing had a left-hand thread.

I'm Getting Older

I see my finish sure and surer,
　　Every year;
For I am getting poor and poorer,
　　Every year;
My wits are getting thicker,
With less capacity for liquor,
　　Every year.

The women, they are sweeter,
　　Every year;
There is more demand for Peter,
　　Every year;
But mine, it gets no bigger,
And it's slower on the trigger,
And cuts less and lesser figure
　　Every year.

FOLK RHYMES

Ring-Dang-Doo

Oh, *Ring-dang-doo!* Pray what is that,
So soft and warm like a pussy cat;
So warm and round, and split in two?
    She said it was her *Ring-dang-doo*.

She took me down into her cellar,
She said I was a damn fine feller;
She fed me wine and whiskey too,
    And let me play with her *Ring-dang-doo*.

"You goddamned fool," her mother said,
"You've gone and broke your maidenhead;
So pack your trunk and suitcase too,
    And go to hell with your *Ring-dang-doo!*"

She went downtown, became a whore,
Hung up a sign outside her door:
"Ten dollars as a start will do,
    To take a crack at my *Ring-dang-doo*."

They came by twos, they came by fours,
Until at last, they came in scores;
But she was glad when they were through,
    For they had wrecked her *Ring-dang-doo*.

And now she lies beneath the sod;
Her soul, they say, is gone to God.
But down in Hell, when Satan's blue,
    He takes a whirl at her *Ring-dang-doo*.

The Last Straw

Life presents a dismal picture,
    Dark and dreary as the tomb:
Father has duodenal stricture;
    Mother, falling of the womb.
Auntie Kate has just aborted,
    For the 42nd time;
Brother Bill has been deported,
    For a homosexual crime.
Cousin George just sits and jerks off,
    Never laughs and never smiles;
Leaves my total occupation
    Cracking ice for grandma's piles.
But we must not be downhearted,
    Nor must we be plagued with doubt—
Sister Jessie has just farted,
    Blown her asshole inside out!

The Tout

The old sport reared in his grandstand chair;
He stroked his whiskers, and tousled his hair;
And his voice rang loud on the sultry air—
  "He'll win in a walk, by Jesus!"

"Just watch his dust when he's turned loose;
He'll go through the field like shit through a goose;
He'll do it as easy as *ace* takes *deuce*—
  He'll win in a walk, by Jesus!"

"His breeding's the best and he *can't* run slow;
He's out of *Black Bess* by *Polarlight Snow;*
His trainer he tells me he's rarin' to go!
  He'll win in a walk, by Jesus!"

FOLK RHYMES

The Tout

"I ain't got much money, but if I was rich——
I'd bet my whole stack on that son-of-a-bitch;
The rest of the starters? He'll give them a hitch!
    He'll win in a walk, by Jesus!"

"They've sent 'em away—he lags at the start——
It don't make no diff'rence—he don't care a fart——
He's bidin' his time—he's got plenty of heart——
    He'll win in a walk, by Jesus!"

"He's in eighth position, way out in the grass,
Where the weeds are so tall that they tickle his ass——
Just a keen sense for drama—that horse is all class!
    He'll win in a walk, by Jesus!"

The Tout

"They're into the stretch, and my boy now is third—
Now he's worked up to second!—Oh! He's slipped on a turd!
He's back in the ditch, the son-of-a-bitch—
     He never was in it, by Jesus!"

The Fair Bather

I knew a young lady at Brighton last year,
Whose hobby was swimming below the long pier.
Each morn she would venture, this trim little lass,
And give you the pleasure of seeing her ——

Antics in the water, in surf, and on sand;
The cutest of all, the belle of the strand.
Her bikini was lovely, the best of the knits,
And displayed to advantage the swell of her——

Trim little figure, which threw me in heat;
That fair little maiden, so lush, so petite.
She never was late, came to the same patch
To enjoy the delight of cooling her——

Self in the water, she'd frolic and play;
Her fun-loving nature was out on display.
She'd float on her side, and for shells she would hunt,
And go through the motions of washing her ——

Clothes out completely and then ring them to dry,
And hang up her undies with langorous sigh.
She could dive like a frog and swim like a duck,
And showed by her motions she knew how to——

Frolic in water, clear up to her chin
Without getting drowned, as so many have been.
Exhausted with swimming, for the shore she would start,
And enjoy the strange pleasure of letting a——

FOLK RHYMES

145

The Fair Bather

Few fellows cast eyes at her beautiful shape
And whistle and stare and hornily gape.
Then she'd dash up the beach she'd decided to quit
And race to the bathhouse to go take a — *shower!*

The Young Man from Calcutta

There was a young man from Calcutta
    Who practiced a curious trick:
He greased up his asshole with buttah
    And therein inserted his prick.

He adopted this measure so shady,
    Not for pleasure, nor power, nor pelf:
But merely because a young lady
    Had told him to go fuck himself.

FOLK RHYMES

Rounding the Horn

For forty days and forty nights
    We sailed the broad Atlantic.
"We must have hide!" the sailors cried;
    The captain, he was frantic!

"We must have tail! Our hearts they fail!"
    The captain did not doubt it.
"Oh, fuck yourselves!" the captain said,
    "And say no more about it!"

"Such sexual fare is but a snare,
    It hasn't helped one bit.
We've buggered days, we've buggered nights;
    Our cocks are caked with shit.

"'Oh, fuck yourselves' you say to us!
    Is that your only answer?
For such grandiloquent advice,
    Your cock should get a cancer!

"We have a yen, we sailor men,
    For cunt juice plain and nasty.
And look at him. Instead of quim,
    He counsels pederasty!

"For forty days and forty nights
    We've bobbed upon this ocean;
We've rocked to fore, we rocked to aft,
    We crave a *screwing* motion."

FOLK RHYMES

Rounding the Horn

The captain gulped; the captain belched;
    His balls gesticulated.
"I'll give you cunt and booze and quim;
    You'll screw till you are sated.

"When we strike shore," the captain swore,
    "I'll buy you luscious whores.
Just cool your chops, till the anchor drops,
    And the fuckin' world is yours!

"So tickle your cocks, till we reach the docks;
    I'll buy you tail by the carlot.
I'll have you fucked, I'll have you sucked,
    Each time by a different harlot."

Rounding the Horn

"'Just cool your chops,   the sailors said,
     "You're pitchin' us a balk.
A set of horny cocks like ours
     Won't just lay down for talk!

"Our tools they swell; they're full of hell;
     They just won't wait 'til shore.
We must have tail! Our hearts they fail!
     We've told you that before.

"And oh! For the poke of a horny spoke
     Into a horny hole.
With a grind and a wind, and a tug and a lug,
     And a screw and a twist and a roll.

FOLK RHYMES

Rounding the Horn

"We've talked of cunt, we've dreamed of cunt,
We must have cunt!" they sang.
"Some words, you'll find, will quiet a mind,
But you just can't still a whang!"

So spake the crew, and without ado,
They all did bare their cocks:
Big stubborn tools, as tough as mules,
And keen and hard as rocks.

The captain saw tumescent clubs,
Each horny as a moose.
"I'm in a fix! What dicks! What pricks!
I see it ain't no use!"

Rounding the Horn

The crew it eyed its captain,
    The captain eyed his crew.
"Unfurl each sail! I'll get you tail.
    In fact—I'll take some, too!"

Hell-bent for screw, that carnal crew,
    Set sail at a fearful rate.
They recked not wind; they recked not gale;
    But reckoned not with fate.

For a terrible storm broke out at sea,
    The ship—its end was near!
On a rockbound coast, Death played the host;
    The captain shit with fear.

FOLK RHYMES

153

Rounding the Horn

But those sailor men, with the horny yen,
    Their heat was not diminished
Till they stubbed their cocks upon the rocks,
    And their dreams of tail were finished!

Toast

A social glass and a social lass
    Go very well together;
But a social lass with a social ass
    I deem a damn sight better.
Here's to the glass, and the lass, and the ass,
    May they meet in all kinds of weather;
We'll drink from the glass, and feel of the ass,
    And make the lass feel better.

FOLK RHYMES

Another Piece

"Now, Bill," she said, "No more tonight;
    You've had a few already."
She was, indeed, a liberal lass;
    But then, he was her steady.

"Ah," Bill replied, foregoing pride,
    "You see, dear, how I crave it;
And, furthermore, what is it for?
    You just don't have to save it."

"Control yourself!" she sweetly said,
    "For soon we will be married.
Control, control will save your soul."
    And that was how she parried.

"Ah! It's so ripe, my angel girl,
    It will not last forever."
She smiled and answered tauntingly,
    "Now don't you think you're clever!"

"Oh, my love! Just one more piece,"
    He pleaded and he pleaded—
"One more won't hurt nor you nor me!"
    She nodded and conceded.

"Okay!" she said, "Okay! Okay!
    You know I can't be mean!"
She took his hand and in it put—
    The remaining tangerine!

FOLK RHYMES

The Unmowed Meadow

One day as I was walking—the month was hot July—
I accosted a young maiden, and she did make reply:
"I have a little meadow that I've kept for you in store,
And 'tis your due to tell you true, it's ne'er been mowed before."

She said, "My handsome gallant, if you a mower be,
I'll give you good employment if you'll come along with me."
So 'twas my great good fortune—Oh! blessed be that town!—
To take my scythe and to contrive to mow her meadow down!

With courage quite undaunted, I stepped out on the ground,
And with my scythe I sure did strive to mow her meadow down.
I mowed from nine 'til dinner time—'twas far beyond my skill—
And then I had to quit the field, but her grass was growing still.

Oh, then that maiden kissed me, again and once again,
"Oh, Sir!" she protested. "You're the greatest of all men!
I'll take to sharpening your scythe, I'll stroke it in my hand,
And then, perhaps, you'll start once more to mow my
meadowland."

The Great Wheel

A man told me before he died—
And I'll never know if the bastard lied—
About his wife who cried and cried
That she'd been never satisfied.

So he built a great big fucking wheel,
A monstrous thing with a prick of steel;
Had two brass balls, all filled with cream,
And the whole friggin' riggin' was driven by steam.

Round and round spun that great big wheel;
And in and out drove that prick of steel;
In and out of that lady's muff,
Until she cried, "Enough! Enough!"

But now we come to the bitter bit:
There was no way of stopping it!
And she began to scream and yell,
But the goddamn thing was bent for hell!

Round and round that wheel did spin,
And drove that prick both out and in.
And she was split from ass to tit,
And the whole friggin' riggin' was covered with shit!

I Had but Fifty Cents

I took my girl out to a ball;
    It was a fancy hop.
At half-past one, the fun was done—
    The music, it did stop.

I took her to a restaurant,
    The best one on the street;
She said she had no appetite,
    But here's what she did eat:

A dozen raw, a bowl of slaw,
    Three hotdogs and a stew;
She ordered shrimp, and I went limp;
    I didn't know what to do!

The waiter asked about dessert—
    I sat by, in suspense;
When she said, "Pie!" I thought I'd die!
    I had but fifty cents.

She said she wasn't thirsty. No!
    She might have "just a sip."
I thought I'd bust; I didn't trust
    Her goddamn cheating lip!

And when she rolled off what she'd have,
    My heart began to sink.
She wasn't one bit thirsty, but
    My God, how she could drink!

FOLK RHYMES

I Had but Fifty Cents

A slug of gin, a glass of *Cin*,
   A mug of lager beer,
A Brandy Alexander, too—
   She made them disappear!

A jug of ale, a pink cocktail—
   Her thirst was just immense.
She ordered more; I hit the floor.
   I had but fifty cents.

I called the boss, asked for my check—
   In came that great big fuck!
I looked sincere, but shat in fear,
   And I gave him my half buck.

I Had but Fifty Cents

He broke my nose, tore up my clothes;
    He stomped me into jelly.
He shoved his fist, up to his wrist,
    Inside my writhing belly.

With obscene calls, he broke my balls,
    My butt was in a sling.
But what I minded most of all
    Was when he whacked my thing!

I stumbled out into the street
    I couldn't drag my ass.
I struggled to my bumbling feet
    Assisted by my lass.

FOLK RHYMES

I Had but Fifty Cents

At last, at last, we both got home;
    She took off all her duds.
Her nipples, sweet, were so petite,
    Like little rosy buds.

'Twas clear she wanted to make up
    I wouldn't play the cad——
She yearned to make some scant amends:
    She'd let herself be had.

She offered me her luscious cunt
    But nothing could avail——
My cock, it wept, but couldn't accept
    That fifty cents of tail.

The Farting Contest

I'll tell you a tale that is sure to please,
Of a grand farting contest at Shitton-on-Pease;
Where all the best farters parade in the fields
To compete in the contest for various shields.

Some tighten their belts and then fart up the scale
To compete for a cup and a barrel of ale;
While others whose asses are biggest and strongest
Compete in the section for loudest and longest.

Now this year's events had drawn a big crowd
And the betting was even on Mrs. McLeod;
For notes had appeared in the evening edition
That this lady's arse was in perfect condition.

FOLK RHYMES

The Farting Contest

Now old Mrs. Jones had a perfect backside,
A forest of hairs with a wart on each side;
And she fancied her chances of winning with ease
Having trained on a diet of cabbage and peas.

The Vicar arrived and ascended the stand,
And thus he addressed this remarkable band:
"The contest is on. As is shown on the bills,
We've precluded the use of injections and pills."

Mrs. Bindle arrived 'mid roars of applause,
And promptly proceeded to pull down her drawers;
And tho she'd no chance in the farting display
She'd the prettiest asshole you'd seen in a day.

The Farting Contest

The ladies lined up. The signal to start
Was given, and Baroness Griper let the first fart.
The people around stood in silence and wonder,
While the radio told of gale warnings and thunder.

Now Mrs. McLeod reckoned nothing of this,
She'd had some weak tea and was all wind and piss;
So she took up her place with her ass opened wide,
But unluckily shit and was disqualified.

Then young Mrs. Pothole was called to the front,
And started by doing a wonderful stunt;
She took a deep breath and clenching her hands
She blew the whole roof off the one shilling stands.

FOLK RHYMES

The Farting Contest

That left Mrs. Bindle who shyly appeared,
And smiled at the clergy who lustily cheered;
And though it was reckoned her chances were small
She wound up the winner, outfarting them all.

With hands on her hips, she stood farting alone;
And the crowd stood amazed at her sweetness of tone;
And the clergy agreed, amid storms of applause,
"You win, Mrs. Bindle! Now pull up your drawers!"

Now with muscles well tensed and her legs full apart
She started a final and glorious fart.
Beginning with Chopin and ending with Bach,
She went right through the classics and wound up with rock.

The Farting Contest

She stood on the rostrum with maidenly gait
And took from the Vicar a set of gold plate;
Then turned to his Worship, with sweetness sublime,
And smilingly said "Come and see me some time!"

FOLK RHYMES

The Tramp Speaks

Don't look at me that way, stranger—
    I didn't shit in your seat;
I've just come down from the mountains,
    And my balls are covered with sleet.

I've been up in the High Sierra—
    Me and me old pal Lou—
A-pimpin' for a whorehouse,
    And a god-damned fine one, too.

'Twas there that I first met Nellie,
    She was the village belle;
I was only a low-down pander,
    But I loved that girl like hell!

Then along comes a city slicker,
    All handsome and gay and rich,
And he stole away my Nellie—
    The stinkin' son-of-a-bitch!

I'm just restin' my ass a moment,
    And then I'm on my way;
I'll get the runt that swiped my cunt,
    If it takes 'til Judgment Day!

The Garter

As I went down to Cornwall, upon a market day,
By chance I spied a lady, a lady on her way;
She was going to market with her butter, eggs, and cream,
So we jogged along together, together on the green.

Jogging with this pretty maid, while jogging by her side,
By chance I spied her garter, her garter was untied;
For fear that she would lose it, I resolved to tell her so—
Says I, "My dear young lady, your garter's hanging low."

"Oh, since you've been so kind, sir; and since you've been so free;
Oh, since you've been so kind, sir, won't you tie it up for me?"
"I will. Oh, yes I will, when we get to yonder hill."
And we jogged along together, together on the green.

Upon our reaching yonder hill, so pleasant was the scene;
On tying up her garter, such a sight was never seen.
She then rolled up her costume, and I rolled me in between,
And we jogged along together, boys, together on the green.

While going out to market, her cream and eggs were sold;
But the losing of her maidenhead, it made her blood run cold;
"Oh, Lord! It's gone! But let it go! The man whom I adore
Is just a fucking son-of-a-bitch, and I'm a little whore."

FOLK RHYMES

Things I Don't Like to See

I'm a modest young man, I'll have you all know;
And I can't bear to hear nor see anything low;
Since childhood, my friends never failed to detect,
That my notions of morals were strictly correct.

I don't like to watch, in a telephone booth,
A girl drop her panties—I deem that uncouth—
Even though the guy standing right next to her there
Has opened his fly, and has loosed his cock bare.

I don't like to see women wearing old smocks;
Nor two fairies at play with each other's cocks.
And I don't like to see—in fact, I abhor—
A girl who's a virgin but talks like a whore!

Now, I don't like to see, no matter 'tis dark,
A clergyman fucking a girl in the park;
Nor I don't like to see—it's not quite elite—
A cute little miss scratch her thing in the street.

I don't like to see, on a bright sunny morn,
A girl with her outfit all crumpled and torn,
Arm in arm with a guy who's had the mishap,
To forget, in his haste, to button his flap.

And I don't like to see, although you might scoff,
An old woman trying to toss herself off.
And while sitting in church, I deem it a shame
To see a chap's hand up the skirt of a dame.

FOLK RHYMES

Things I Don't Like to See

The fact is that while I sit there in my pew
There are many strange things that come into view:
Just last Sunday morning the white of an egg
Ran down the pants of a young curate's leg.

I fear I'm encroaching too much on your time,
And so I will end this confessional rhyme.
Though my taste is quite strange, you'll often agree,
I've told you the things that I don't like to see.

The Civil Whore

The Postman came
    On the first of May;
The Policeman came
    The very next day;
Nine months later
    There was hell to pay;
Who fired the shot?
    The Blue or the Gray?

FOLK RHYMES

Two Virgin Lads

Two lads were out on Hertford Heath
    And being flush o' money;
They offered two bob to a wench
    To let them view her cunny.

They peered at it with great delight,
    Stark naked and provoking;
They paid their shillings for the sight,
    The touching and the stroking.

"Now," said the brazen little slut,
    "For just a half-crown each,
I'll let your cocks into my slit,
    As far as they can reach."

She took the taller by the arm,
　　"I'll guide you with my hand."
Alas! the lad shot off before
　　He reached the Promised Land!

The second boy was beckoned, and
　　She gently touched his thing;
Scarce reached the golden portal when
　　His prick it spurted—Zing!

She sensed both lads were much let down;
　　No fucking, yet had spent!
"Well,"quoth she , "you both did right;
　　Today, you know, starts Lent!"

FOLK RHYMES

Blinded by Turds

There was an old lady,
　　I'd have you know;
Who went up to London
　　A short time ago.
The neighbors were tickled
　　When she went away.
But that lady liked London,
　　Decided to stay.

Now when this fat lady
　　Retired one night;
She said, 'Oh, my gawd!
　　I just have to shite!"
Now this fat lady
　　Was a ponderous lass.
She went to the window
　　And out went her ass.

There was an old watchman
	Who chanced to pass by;
Looked up, got a chunk
	Right square in the eye.
He put up his hand
	To see where he was hit.
And he said, "Oh, my gawd!
	I'm blinded with shit!"

Now this poor watchman
	Was done for, for life.
He had five pretty children
	And a fine fuckin' wife.
On a London street corner
	Mark well the words!
There's a sign on his chest
	Which reads, BLINDED BY TURDS.

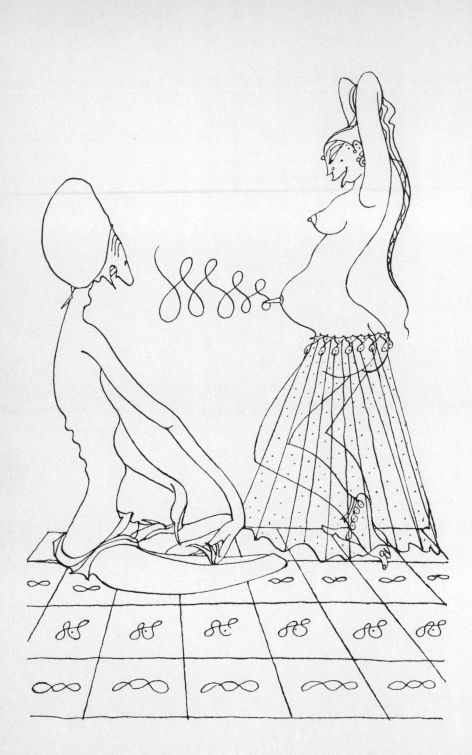

RESPONSA

MOTHER: Has the iceman come yet?

DAUGHTER: No, but he's breathing hard.

❖   ❖   ❖

AIRLINE HOSTESS: Would you like some of our special TWA coffee?

PASSENGER: No, but I'd love some of your TWA tea.

❖   ❖   ❖

MIDGET TO PRETTY GIRL: What do you say to a little fuck?

PRETTY GIRL: Hello, little fuck.

❖   ❖   ❖

IRATE HOUSEWIFE: My husband can lick your husband.

SECOND HOUSEWIFE: I think he does.

❖   ❖   ❖

HIPPIE: Have you ever been picked up by the fuzz?

FLOWER CHICK: No, but I bet it hurts like crazy.

SUNDAY SCHOOL TEACHER: (admonishingly) Do you know where little girls and boys go when they do bad things?

LITTLE BOY: Back of Shannon's garage.

❈   ❈   ❈

ITALIAN GUIDE: We are now passing the most fabulous brothel in Rome.

MALE TOURIST: Why?

❈   ❈   ❈

YOUNG MAN: Is that Hortense?

GIRL FRIEND: She looks relaxed to me.

❈   ❈   ❈

EUROPEAN: You know, I come from the other side.

GIRL FRIEND: Gee, that I gotta see!

❈   ❈   ❈

CUSTOMER: What's your ceiling price?

PROSTITUTE: Same as on the floor.

BOSOMY TICKET AGENT: What'll you have, sir?

GOGGLEYED STUDENT: I want two pickets for Tittsburgh.

✳　✳　✳

YOUNG DAUGHTER: Mommy, what's the difference between a snowman and a snowwoman?

MOTHER: Snowballs, my darling.

✳　✳　✳

BRIDE-TO-BE: I should use orange juice for birth control? When should I take it—before or after?

DOCTOR: Neither. Instead!

✳　✳　✳

CENSUS TAKER: Kinfolk?

YOUNG SWEET THING: I kin folk a little.

✳　✳　✳

PSYCHOLOGIST: Do you cheat on your wife?

PATIENT: Who else?

HE: (pouring a drink) Say when.

SHE: After this drink.

❋ ❋ ❋

DOCTOR: (taking up his stethoscope) Big breaths.

GIRL: Yeth, and I'm not thixteen yet.

❋ ❋ ❋

FIRST MORON: It's very nice out tonight.

SECOND MORON: Yes. I think I'll take mine out too.

❋ ❋ ❋

OLD ROGUE: There may be winter in my hair, but there's summer in my heart.

YOUNG DEAR: Yes, but is there any spring in your ass?

❋ ❋ ❋

EXCITED HUSBAND: Quick, Mary, I just got my semi-annual hard-on.

INCREDULOUS WIFE: You mean you just got your annual semi-hard-on.

Ribald Songs

The Bastard King of England

Oh, the bards they sing of an Eng-lish king Who

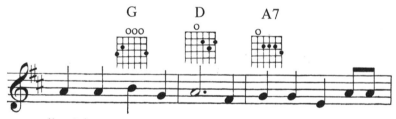

lived long years a - go; He ruled the land with an

i - ron hand, But his   mind was weak and

low.   He__ used to bag the__

roy - al stag With__ which his woods were

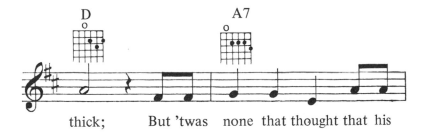

thick;   But 'twas none that thought that his

The Bastard King of England

fav'-rite sport Was   pull-ing the roy-al   prick.

Oh, the bards they sing of an English king
    Who lived long years ago;
He ruled the land with an iron hand,
    But his mind was weak and low.
He used to bag the royal stag
    With which his woods were thick;
But 'twas none that thought that his fav'rite sport
    Was pulling the royal prick.

The Bastard King of England

And his nether garb was a woolen shirt
    Which he used to hide his hide;
But this undershirt couldn't hide the dirt
    That no one could abide.
He was wild and woolly and full of fleas
    That humans ne'er could stand;
And his terrible dong hung down to his knees—
    The Bastard King of England.

Now the Queen of Spain was an amorous dame,
    A sprightly dame was she;
And she longed to fool with His Majesty's tool,
    So far across the sea.
So she sent a note to the dirty King
    By her royal messenger;
And begged his liege to sail to Spain
    To spend a month with her.

The Bastard King of England

When the Spanish King was told this thing,
    He said to all his court:
"My lousy Queen ain't comin' clean
    Because my tool is short."
So to Britain's shores he shipped three whores
    —It was a clever trap!—
To lure that boor, and fix him sure,
    With a royal dose of clap.

When the news of this filthy deed was heard
    In Windsor's merry halls,
The King took oath he would have both
    Of the Frenchman's greasy balls.
So he offered the half of all his lands,
    And the whole of Queen Lorraine,
To that trusty lord of his English court
    Who'd nut the King of Spain.

The Bastard King of England

So the royal Duke of Essexshire
 Betook himself to sea;
And he laid in wait at the privy gate
 When the King went out to pee.
Then around his prong, he tied a thong
 And gaily galloped along;
'Til at last in Windsor's merry halls
 Was the Spaniard and his dong.

But the Bastard King gained not a thing
 For in the lengthy ride,
The thong had stretched by a yard or more
 The fucking Spaniard's pride.
Then all the ladies of London town
 Who saw that mighty stand
Cried: "To hell and down with the English crown!"
 And made Phillip King of England.

Chicago

I   used   to work in Chi - ca - go,

In a de - part - ment store;   I

used   to work in Chi - ca - go,   I

did but I don't no more.　　　A

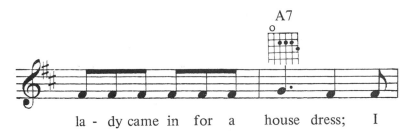

la - dy came in for a house dress;　I

asked her what kind she wore.

"Jump-er!" she said. And jump 'er I did,And I

don't work there an - y - more.

I used to work in Chicago,
    In a department store;
I used to work in Chicago,
    I did but I don't no more.
A lady came in for a house dress;
    I asked her what kind she wore.
"Jumper!" she said. And jump 'er I did—
    And I don't work there anymore!

Chicago

I used to work in Chicago,
    In a department store;
I used to work in Chicago,
    I did but I don't no more.
A lady came in for a girdle;
    I asked her what kind she wore.
"Rubber!" she said. And rub 'er I did—
    And I don't work there anymore!

I used to work in Chicago,
    In a downtown bakery store;
I used to work in Chicago,
    I did but I don't no more.
A lady came in for a sponge cake;
    I asked her what kind she wished.
"Layer!" she said. And lay 'er I did—
    And I don't work there anymore!

Chicago

I used to work in Chicago,
    In a millinery store;
I used to work in Chicago,
    I did but I don't no more.
A lady came in to buy a hat;
    I asked her what kind she wore.
"Felt!" she said. And that's how she left—
    And I don't work there anymore!

I used to work in Chicago,
    In a travel agency store;
I used to work in Chicago,
    I did but I don't no more.
A lady came in for a ticket;
    I asked where she wanted to go.
"Bangor!" she said. And bang 'er I did—
    And I don't work there anymore!

Chicago

I used to work in Chicago,
    In a great big pet store;
I used to work in Chicago,
    I did but I don't no more.
A lady came in to buy a pet;
    I asked her what she had in mind.
"A pussy!" she said. And I took the hint—
    And I don't work there anymore!

I used to work in Chicago,
    In a great big dairy store;
I used to work in Chicago,
    I did but I don't no more.
A lady came in wanting dairies;
    I asked her what she wished
"Cream!" she said. And cream her I did—
    And I don't work there anymore!

The Winnepeg Whore

My first trip up the Chip-pe-way Riv - er

took me eight - y miles up shore;

There I met a young Miss Flan - ni - gan,

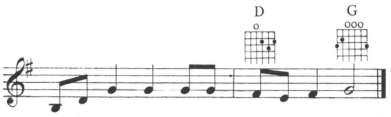

Com-mon-ly known as "The Win - ni - peg Whore."

My first trip up the Chippeway River,
  Took me 80 miles up shore;
There I met a young Miss Flannigan,
  Commonly known as "The Winnipeg Whore."

"Well," says she to me, "I think I know you, boy;
  Let me sit upon your knee.
How's about a little lovin'?
  A dollar and a half is the usual fee."

The Winnepeg Whore

Well, I took her on, and she led me
    Quickly to the place where she used to sleep;
Dirty old room with a straw-filled mattress,
    Wasn't too clean, but she sure was cheap.

Oh, she was slick as a slippery elm;
    I didn't know what she was about,
'Til I missed my watch and wallet.
    "Holy Moses!" I cried out.

Then up to the whore's ran some sons-of-bitches
    Up to the tune of 15 or more.
I left my clothes, my shoes, and my britches
    And I went a-high-tailin' out of that door!

The Winnepeg Whore

Yes, in Winnipeg I learned my lesson,
    I learned it good 'cause I learned it there;
If you got to visit a Winnipeg whore, boys,
    Better make sure that you visit her bare.

In the Shade of the Old Apple Tree

In the shade of the old ap - ple tree,___

___ I got all that was com - ing to me.___

In the soft dew - y grass, I had

my piece of ass From a maid-en that

was fine to see.____ I could hear the dull

buzz of the bee ____ As it sunk its grub

In the Shade of the Old Apple Tree

hooks in - to me.____ Her ass it was

fine, but you should have seen mi -ne-- In the

shade of the old ap - ple tree.____

In the Shade of the Old Apple Tree

In the shade of the old apple tree,
I got all that was coming to me.
    In the soft dewy grass, I had my piece of ass
From a maiden that was fine to see.

I could hear the dull buzz of the bee
As it sunk its grub hooks into me.
    Her ass it was fine, but you should have seen mine—
In the shade of the old apple tree.

No Balls at All

Oh, come all ye lad-dies and lis-ten to
me, And I'll tell you a tale that will fill you with
glee; Of a pret-ty young maid-en so fair and so

tall, Who mar-ried a man who had no balls at all!

Chorus

No balls at all; no balls at all; She

mar-ried a man who had no balls at all!

No Balls at All

No balls at all; no balls at all;
She married a man who had no balls at all!

Oh, come all ye laddies and listen to me,
And I'll tell you a tale that will fill you with glee;
Of a pretty young maiden so fair and so tall,
Who married a man who had no balls at all!

The night of the wedding she crept into bed;
Her cheeks were so rosy, her ass was so red.
She reached for his penis, his penis was small;
She reached for his balls, but he'd no balls at all!

"Oh, Mother! Oh, Mother! Oh, what shall I do?
I've married a man who's unable to screw.
My troubles are many, my pleasures are small,
For I've married a man who has no balls at all!"

No Balls at All

"Oh, daughter! Oh, daughter! Do not be so sad;
The same thing was true when I married your dad.
But there's always a good man awaiting the call
Of the wife of a man who has no balls at all!"

This very wise daughter took mother's advice;
She got herself laid by a man who seemed nice.
And a queer looking bastard was born in the fall,
To the wife of the man who had no balls at all!

The husband was joyous; got high as a kite;
The sight of that infant filled him with delight!
Though its head was too large, and its body too small,
The great thing about him—he'd no balls at all!

Her Name Was Lil

Her name was Lil, and she was a beau-ty; She
lived in a house of ill re - pu - tee. The
men all came from far to see

Lil - i - an   in   her   des - ha - bille.

Lil - ian   in   her   des   -   ha - bille!

Her name was Lil, and she was a beauty;
She lived in a house of ill reputee.
The men all came from far to see
Lilian in her deshabille.
  Lilian in her deshabille!

Her Name Was Lil

She was comely, she was fair,
She had lovely yellow hair.
But she drank too much of the demon rum,
And she smoked hashish and opium.
    And she smoked hashish and opium!

Now, day by day her cheeks grew thinner
Because of the lack of protein in her.
She grew two hollows in her chest
'Til she had to go 'round completely dressed.
    'Til she had to go 'round completely dressed!

She went to see the house physician
To prescribe for her condition.
"You have got," the doctors say,
"Per-nish-i-us anem-i-a.
    Per-nish-i-us anem-i-a!"

Her Name Was Lil

She took treatments in the sun,
She tried Scott's emul-si-on.
Three times daily she took yeast,
But still her clientele decreased.
   But still her clientele decreased!

Now it may be said of her cli-en-telly,
That it rested mainly on her belly.
And when she covered herself with cloth,
Her clientele grew exceeding wroth.
   Her clientele grew exceedingly wroth!

Now clothes may make a girl go far,
But they have no place on a *fille de joie;*
And Lily's troubles they began
When she concealed her ab-do-men.
   When she concealed her abdomen!

Her Name Was Lil

As she lay there in her dishonor
She felt the hand of the Lord upon her.
She said, "Oh, Lord, I do repent,
But that feel's gonna cost you fifty cents."
   But that feel's gonna cost you fifty cents!"

The Spanish Nobilio

There once was a Span-ish no -

bi-li - o,_____ Who lived in an an-cient cas-

til - li - o;_____ He was proud of his

The Spanish Nobilio

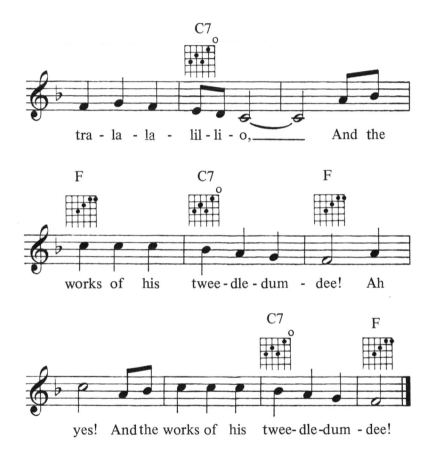

tra - la - la - lil - li - o,_____ And the

works of his twee - dle - dum - dee! Ah

yes! And the works of his twee - dle - dum - dee!

The Spanish Nobilio

There once was a Spanish nobilio,
Who lived in an ancient castillio;
He was proud of his tra-la-la-lillio,
    And the works of his tweedle-dum-dee!

One day he went to the theatillio,
And there saw a lovely dancillio
Who excited his tra-la-la-lillio,
    And the works of his tweedle-dum-dee!

He took her up to his castillio
And laid her upon his sofillio,
Then inserted his tra-la-la-lillio,
    And the works of his tweedle-dum-dee!

The Spanish Nobilio

Nine days later he saw the doctillio;
He had a fine dose of clapillio
All over his tra-la-la-lillio,
    And the works of his tweedle-dum-dee!

Now he sits in his ancient castillio,
With a handful of cotton-wadillio,
And swabs off his tra-la-la-lillio,
    And the works of his tweedle-dum-dee!

Redwing

There once was an In - dian maid   Who was

ver - y much a - fraid   That some buck-a-roo Would

slip it up her sloo   As she lay in the shade. She

Redwing

had an i-dea grand: She filled her slit with

sand;   So   no   buck-a-roo Would

slip it   up her sloo With - out her get-ting

Redwing

paid.   Oh, the moon shines down on pret-ty

Red - wing,   As she lies sleep - ing,

There comes a - creep - ing,   A pair of

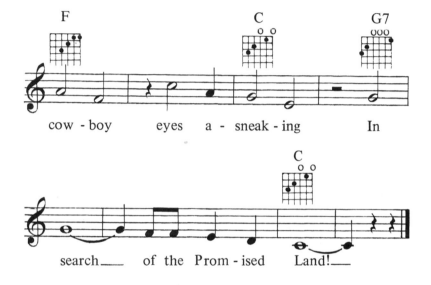

cow - boy eyes a - sneak - ing In

search___ of the Prom - ised Land!___

There once was an Indian maid

Who was very much afraid

That some buckaroo

Would slip it up her sloo

As she lay in the shade.

Redwing

She had an idea grand:
She filled her slit with sand;
    So no buckaroo
    Would slip it up her sloo
Without her getting paid.

Oh, the moon shines down on pretty Redwing,
    As she lies sleeping,
    There comes a-creeping,
    A pair of cowboy eyes a-sneaking
        In search of the *Promised Land!*

Now this buckaroo was wise,
He crept between her thighs;
    He seemed so cute
    With his swelled up root
As he went for the *Promised Land.*

Redwing

Little Redwing came to life,
She drew her bowie knife;
    With one quick pass
    She cut his balls from his ass—
And his sporting days were past.

Oh the sun shines down on pretty Redwing;
    As she lies snoring,
    There hangs a warning;
    A pair of cowboy balls adorning
        The flap of her wigwam door!

Zulaika

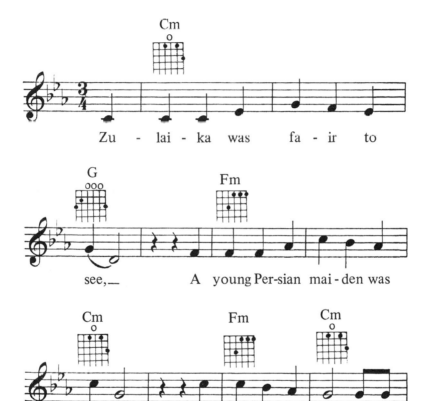

Zu - lai - ka was fa - ir to see, ___ A young Per-sian mai - den was she - ee. She lived in Bagh - dad, And she

Zulaika

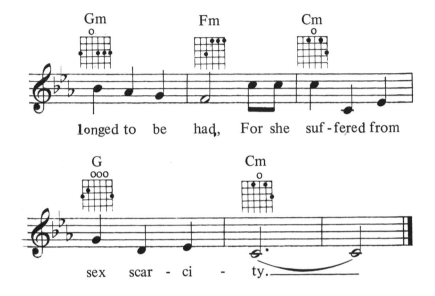

longed to be had, For she suf-fered from

sex scar - ci - ty.____

Zulaika was fair to see,
A young Persian maiden was she.
She lived in Baghdad,
And she longed to be had,
For she suffered from sex scarcity.

Zulaika

Her husband was very old,
With millions in silver and gold.
    He kept her locked in
    Away from all sin
But she vowed she'd get out of the cold.

Zulaika was nobody's fool,
She intended to play it all cool.
    She concocted a plan
    To get her a man
Who at least had a practical tool.

On her belly she wound a turban,
And around her thighs it ra-an,
    And inside her wee-wee,
    She hid a small key
Which she threw out a-gan and a-gan.

Zulaika

Well, the first time she threw out the key
It fell near the handsome Ali.
  She sighed and she cried,
  And the door opened wide,
And in walked her lover-to-be.

Next week she tried once a-gan,
And a riot almost began.
  When the door opened wide,
  There stood, side by side,
Six guys who claimed he was the man!

Then she prayed to the gods of Iran,
And threw out the key once a-gan.
  She sighed and she cried,
  And the door opened wide,
And in trooped a whole caravan.

Zulaika

Now the leader he bowed his head low,
And waited, her wishes to know.
  "Well, most of you stay,"
  Zulaika did say—
"But the children and camels must go!"

That Little Ball of Yarn

It was in the month of May, When the jacks be-gin to bray, And the jen-nies come pran-cing a - round the barn; Said the

jen-nie to the jack, "Will you climb up-on my

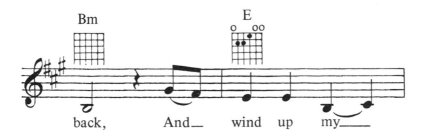

back, And__ wind up my___

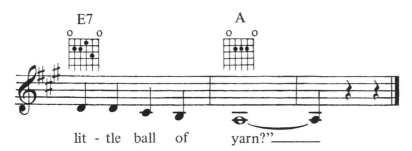

lit - tle ball of yarn?"_____

That Little Ball of Yarn

It was in the month of May,
When the jacks begin to bray,
    And the jennies come prancing around the barn;
Said the jennie to the jack,
"Will you climb upon my back,
    And wind up my little ball of yarn?"

It was in the month of June,
When the whole world was in tune,
    And the violets were smiling 'round the barn;
There I met a little Miss,
And I simply asked her this:
    "May I wind up your little ball of yarn?"

That Little Ball of Yarn

Said she, "Just go to those,
Who have money and fine clothes;
    Why don't you go to them with all your charms?"
But she finally gave consent,
And through the fields we went,
    A-planning to wind up her ball of yarn!

Soon we found the proper spot,
And her cheeks grew very hot,
    As I asked her to unfold her little charm;
Then I gently laid her down,
And she bade me lift her gown,
    And I wound up her little ball of yarn!

That Little Ball of Yarn

It was nine months after that,
In my office chair I sat,
    A-wondering had I done her any harm;
When appeared before the door,
Her old man who gave a roar,
    "You're the daddy of a little ball of yarn!"

From the look in his left eye,
I could tell he didn't lie,
    Her old man wasn't spinning me a yarn.
So I knew my goose was cooked;
 And since that day I've been hooked—
    A-winding up that selfsame ball of yarn!

The Ball at Kerrimuir

They all came down to Ker-ri-muir, There
was a great big ball, There al-so was a
wed - ding, But that ain't tell - in' all. Oh!

The Ball at Kerrimuir

Please do it this time, Oh! Please do it now! And

if you did it last time, You surely must know how!

Who of us will e'er forget
The ball at Kerrimuir,
Where your wife and my wife
Wound up on the floor.

The Ball at Kerrimuir

CHORUS

Oh! Please do it this time,
Oh! Please do it now!
And if you did it last time,
You surely must know how!

Five and twenty virgins came
    Down from Inverness;
And when the ball was over
    There were five and twenty less.

First lady forward;
    Second lady back;
Third lady's finger
    Up fourth lady's crack.

The Ball at Kerrimuir

Oh, there was fuckin' in the parlor,
    And fuckin' in the ricks;
You couldn't hear the music for
    The swishin' of the pricks.

Oh, there was fuckin' on the porches,
    And fuckin' on the stones;
You couldn't hear the music for
    The groanin' and the moans.

Oh, there was fuckin' in the kitchen,
    And fuckin' on the stairs;
You couldn't see the carpets for
    The cunts and curly hairs.

The Ball at Kerrimuir

The bride was in the bedroom
    Explainin' to the groom—
That the vagina, not the rectum,
    Was the entrance to the womb.

The Queen was in the parlor
    Eatin' bread and honey;
The King was in the chambermaid,
    And she was in the money.

Oh, the minister's daughter she was there,
    She had them all in fits,
Jumpin' off the mantlepiece
    And bouncin' off her tits.

The Ball at Kerrimuir

The village cripple he was there,
    I didn't like him much;
He lined two girls against the wall
    And fucked them with his crutch.

Jimmie Brown he was there,
    Up to every trick;
Dancin' naked 'round the floor
    And standin' on his prick.

Plowin' Jock he was there,
    The bugger wouldn't dance;
Sat sittin' with a hard-on
    Just a-waitin' for his chance!

The Ball at Kerrimuir

Tommy Reid he was there,
    His balls were made of brass;
And when he blew a fart, my lads,
    The sparks flew out his ass.

The hostler's wife she was there
    A-sittin' down in front;
A ring of roses in her hair
    And a carrot up her cunt.

The village idiot he was there
    A-makin' like a fool;
He pulled his foreskin o'er his head
    And whistled through his tool.

The Ball at Kerrimuir

Jack Todd was in the bathroom
    Countin' up his wealth;
His wife was in the bedroom
    A-diddlin' with herself.

Fat McTavish she was there,
    She looked just like a sow;
They tied her by the red barn door
    And bulled her like a cow.

The parson's wife she was there,
    And she was worst of all;
She pulled her skirt above her head,
    And shouted, "Fuck it all!"

The Ball at Kerrimuir

The Thompson boys they were there
    And they were quite a pair—
Each fucked a lassie seven times
    And never touched the hair.

The village blacksmith he was there,
    He played a wily game;
He fucked his lassie fourteen times
    Before he fin'lly came.

Postman Simpson he was there,
    And he'd a dose of pox;
He couldn't fuck the women
    So he fucked the letter-box.

The Ball at Kerrimuir

The deacon's wife was standin' there,
    Her butt against the wall—
"Put your money on the table, boys,
    I'm goin' to do youse all!"

Dr. Sangster he was there,
    At surgery, he was grand;
He took most of the evening
    To circumcize the band.

Oh, the tailor was a busy man,
    The work went to his head—
Sewin' up the torn cunts with
    Miles and miles of thread!

The Ball at Kerrimuir

It started out so simple-like
    Each lass and laddie mated;
But pretty soon the fuckin' got
    So fuckin' complicated.

And when the ball was over,
    The girls did all suggest;
They sure enjoyed the music, but
    The fuckin' was the best!

The Shithouse Rag

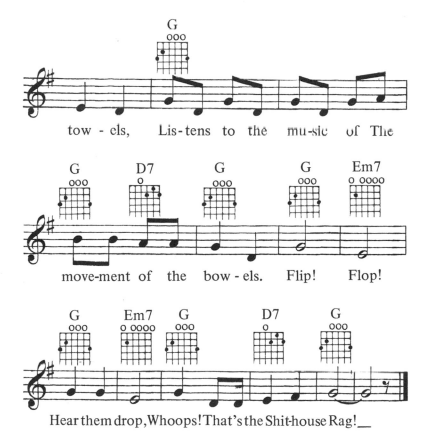

tow - els, Lis-tens to the mu-sic of The

move-ment of the bow - els. Flip! Flop!

Hear them drop, Whoops! That's the Shit-house Rag!__

The Shithouse Rag

Sam! Sam! The Shithouse Man!
Superintendent of the crappery can.
    Picks up the papers,
    Folds up the towels,
    Listens to the music of
    The movement of the bowels.
    Flip! Flop!
    Hear them drop!
Whoops!—That's the *Shithouse Rag!*

My Sweet Little Alice Blue Gown

Was the first time I ev - er layed

In my sweet lit - tle A - lice Blue gown

down;— I was both proud and shy as he

Alice Blue Gown

o - pened his fly, And the mo -ment I

saw it — I thought I would die! Oh, it

hung al - most down to the ground;—

Alice Blue Gown

As it went in, I made not a sound;___ Oh, the more that he shoved it, the more did I love it, As he

Alice Blue Gown

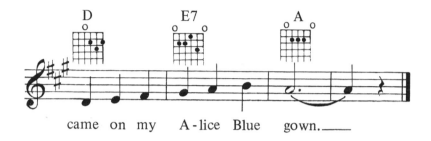

came on my A-lice Blue gown.____

In my sweet little Alice Blue gown,
Was the first time I ever layed down;
    I was both proud and shy as he opened his fly,
And the moment I saw it—I thought I would die!

Oh, it hung almost down to the ground;
As it went in, I made not a sound.
    Oh, the more that he shoved it, the more did I love it,
As he came on my Alice Blue gown.

The Freshmen up at Yale

Oh, the fresh-men up at Yale get no

tail, *get no tail*; Oh, the fresh-men up at

Yale get no tail, *get no tail*; So for

The Freshmen up at Yale

want of re - cre - a - tion They in - dulge in mas-tur -

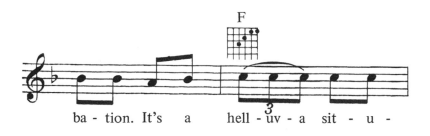

ba - tion. It's a hell -uv - a sit - u -

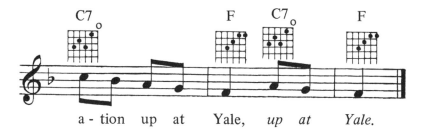

a - tion up at Yale, *up at Yale.*

The Freshmen up at Yale

Oh, the freshmen up at Yale get no tail, get no tail;
Oh, the freshmen up at Yale get no tail, get no tail;
　　So for want of recreation
　　They indulge in masturbation;
It's a helluva situation up at Yale, up at Yale.

Oh, the eagles they fly high in Mobile,
Oh, the eagles they fly high in Mobile;
　　Oh, the eagles they fly high;
　　And they shit right in your eye—
Oh, it's good the cows don't fly in Mobile!

The Freshmen up at Yale

Oh, if you are put in jail in Mobile,
Oh, if you are put in jail in Mobile;
    Oh, if you are put in jail,
    And you need a piece of tail—
Oh, the sheriff's wife's for sale in Mobile.

Lydia Pinkham

Let us sing__ of Lyd-i-a Pink-ham, And her love for the hu-man race; How she sells__ her *Vege-ta-ble Com-pound*, And the

Lydia Pinkham

pa - pers pub-lish her face.   So let us

sing, sing, sing of Lyd-i - a Pink-ham, And her

love   for the hu -man race;   How she

Lydia Pinkham

sells, sells, sells her *Vege-ta-ble Com-pound,* And the

pa - pers pub-lish her face.

Let us sing of Lydia Pinkham,
    And her love for the human race;
How she sells her *Vegetable Compound,*
    And the papers publish her face.

Lydia Pinkham

So let us sing, sing, sing of Lydia Pinkham,
And her love for the human race;
How she sells, sells, sells her Vegetable Compound,
And the papers publish her face.

Oh! It sells for a dollar a bottle,
And it cures all manner of ills;
And it's more to be recommended
Than Carter's Liver Pills.

Widow Brown she had no children,
Though she loved them very dear;
So she took some *Vegetable Compound,*
Now she has them twice a year!

Lydia Pinkham

Willy Sanders, the little fuck-up,
    Could pass no water—none at all!
So we gave him three bottles of *Compound*—
    Now he clears a ten-foot wall!

Walter Black had a terrible problem,
    For his pecker wouldn't peck;
Then he took some *Vegetable Compound*—
    Now he fucks 'til he's a wreck!

Mary Bender had no breastworks,
    And she couldn't fill her blouse;
So she took some *Vegetable Compound,*
    Now they milk her with the cows!

Lydia Pinkham

Johnny Winters, the little bastard,
  Through masturbation lost his vim;
So we gave him two bottles of *Compound*,
  Now the rabbits envy him!

Arthur White had been castrated,
  Hadn't even a single nut;
So he took some *Vegetable Compound*,
  Now six balls hang 'round his butt.

Father Francis couldn't marry;
  Never felt a tit or twat;
Since we gave him some *Vegetable Compound*,
  His wet dreams could fill a pot!

Lydia Pinkham

Sally Jones had rotten kidneys;
  Poor old lady couldn't pee;
So she took some *Vegetable Compound*,
  Now they pipe her out to sea!

Do Your Balls Hang Low?

Do your balls hang low? Do they

wig-gle to and fro? Can you tie 'em in a

knot? Can you tie 'em in a bow? If you

got a wee bit bold-er, could you sling 'em on your

shoul-der? *Do your balls hang low?*____

Do your balls hang low? Do they wiggle to and fro?
Can you tie 'em in a knot? Can you tie 'em in a bow?
If you got a wee bit bolder, could you sling 'em on your shoulder?
  Do your balls hang low?

Do Your Balls Hang Low?

Do your balls hang low? Can you swing 'em in an arc?
Can you sit astride your genitals and roll through Central Park?
Can you juggle 'em in tune, to the rhythm of "High Noon"?
  Do your balls hang low?

Aboard the Good Ship Venus

A - board the good ship Ve - nus, My

God! You should have seen us! The fi-gure-head was a

whore in bed, And the mast a ram -pant pe- nis!

Aboard the Good Ship Venus

Aboard the good ship Venus,
My God! You should have seen us!
  The figurehead was a whore in bed—
And the mast, a rampant penis!

The captain of this lugger,
He was a dirty bugger;
  He wasn't fit to shovel shit
From one place to another!

The first mate's name was Andy,
He acted like a dandy;
  We fixed that shite—we fixed him right—
By pissin' in his brandy!

Aboard the Good Ship Venus

The bosun had a daughter
Who fell into the water;
  Delighted squeals revealed that eels
Had found her sexual quarter.

The Captain's wife was Mabel;
Whenever she was able,
  She'd fornicate the second mate
Upon the galley table.

The galley mate was Ryan,
And always he was dyin'
  To lick the tits of Sailor Fritz;
But Fritz—he wasn't buyin'!

Aboard the Good Ship Venus

The purser's wife was Gussie,
A great gal but a hussy;
    For just one buck, she'd squat and suck
The nurse's little pussy.

Aboard the good ship Venus
We sailors all were heinous;
    It was our fate to masturbate—
And that develops meanness.

One day the good ship foundered,
On crags our bags were pounded;
    We stubbed our cocks against the rocks—
And then we all were drownded!

The Chisholm Trail

I reached in my pock-et, and I pulled out a pen-ny. She says, "For that you won't get an-y!" So go tie your

RIBALD SONGS

The Chisholm Trail

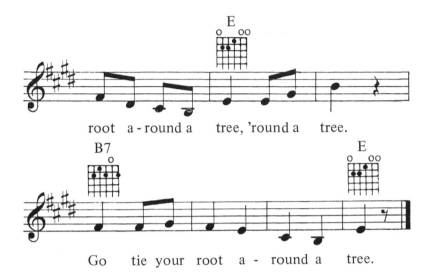

root a - round a   tree, 'round a   tree.

Go   tie your root a - round a   tree.

I reached in my pocket, and I pulled out a penny.
She says, "For that you won't get any!"

CHORUS

So go tie your root around a tree,
'Round a tree. Go tie your root around a tree.

The Chisholm Trail

I reached in my pocket, and I pulled out a nickle.
She says, "For that you won't get a tickle!"

I reached in my pocket, and I pulled out a dime.
She says, "For that you're wasting your time!"

I reached in my pocket, and I pulled out a quarter.
She says, "Young man! I'm a minister's daughter!"

I reached in my pocket, and I pulled out a half.
She didn't even talk—just started to laugh!

I reached in my pocket, and I pulled out a dollar.
She took my money, and she opened her collar.

The Chisholm Trail

So I reached in my pocket and pulled out a five.
She said, "Come inside; we'll see if you're alive!"

Well, I rode her standin', and I rode her lyin',
And if I had wings, I'd have rode her flyin'!

Well, I went to the doctor 'cause my rod was sore.
"Good Lord!" said the doctor. "It's that same fuckin' whore!

"You can put away your holster, and put away your gun;
Your barrel's been breached, and your shootin' days are done!"

Humoresque

Pas - sen - gers will please re - frain, From

flush - ing toi - lets while the train Is

in the sta - tion. Dar - ling, I love

Humoresque

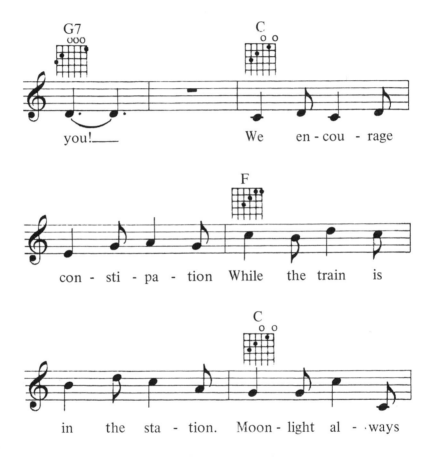

you!___ We en - cou - rage con - sti - pa - tion While the train is in the sta - tion. Moon - light al - ways

Humoresque

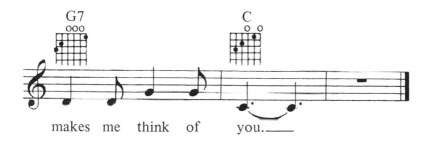

makes   me   think   of   you.____

Passengers will please refrain
From flushing toilets while the train
   Is in the station. Darling, I love you!
We encourage constipation
While the train is in the station.
   Moonlight always makes me think of you.

Humoresque

If the ladies' room is taken,
Never feel the least foresaken,
    Never show a sign of sad defeat.
Try the men's room in the hall,
And if some man has had the call,
    He'll courteously relinquish you his seat.

If these efforts are in vain,
Then simply break a windowpane—
    A novel method used by very few.
My occupation after dark
Is goosing statues in the park;
    If Sherman's horse can take it, why can't you?

If you wish to pass some water,
Kindly call the pullman porter,
    He'll place the vessel in the vestibule.
If the porter isn't here,
Try the platform in the rear —
    The one in the front is likely to be full.

My God!
How the Money Rolls In!

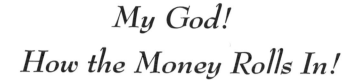

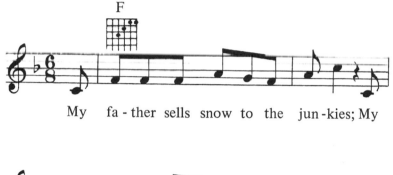

My   fa - ther sells snow to the   jun - kies; My

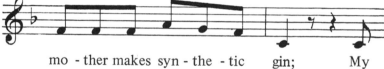

mo - ther makes syn - the - tic   gin;   My

sis - ter makes love for   a   liv - ing;   My

My God! How the Money Rolls In!

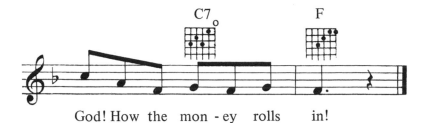

God! How the mon - ey rolls in!

My father sells snow to the junkies;
    My mother makes synthetic gin;
My sister makes love for a living.
    My God! How the money rolls in!

My grandma's a boarding house keeper;
    She takes little working girls in;
She put a red light in the window.
    And God! How the money rolls in!

My God! How the Money Rolls In!

My brother's a big social worker;
    He studies feminine sin;
He'll land you a blonde for ten dollars.
    My God! How the money rolls in!

My uncle he dabbles in numbers,
    As well as in poker and gin;
He knows how to deal from the bottom.
    And God! How the money rolls in!

My aunt runs a fine seminary,
    To give girls a cultural in;
The callers address her as "Madam."
    My God! How the money rolls in!

Roll Me Over in the Clover

Now— this is Num-ber One, And the fun has just be - gun! Roll me o - ver, lay me down, and do it a - gain.— Now—

this is Num-ber Two;Please ac -cept my thanks to

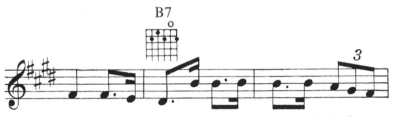

you. Roll me   o - ver,lay me   down and do it a-

gain.___ *Roll me   o - ver   in   the   clo -*

Roll Me Over in the Clover

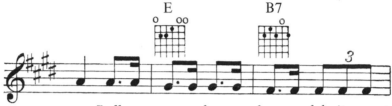

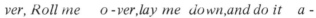

ver, Roll me   o -ver,lay me   down,and do it   a -

gain.____   Roll me   o - ver   in   the

clo -   ver; Roll   me   o - ver, lay   me

Roll Me Over in the Clover

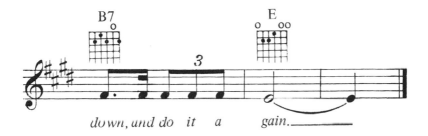

down, and do it a gain._____

Now this is Number One—
And the fun has just begun!
 Roll me over, lay me down, and do it again.
Now this is Number Two—
Please accept my thanks to you.
 Roll me over, lay me down, and do it again.

CHORUS

Roll me over in the clover;
Roll me over, lay me down, and do it again.

Roll Me Over in the Clover

Now this is Number Three—
And I'm fuckin' fancy free!
 Roll me over, lay me down, and do it again.
Now this is Number Four—
I know what my pussy's for!
 Roll me over, lay me down, and do it again.

Now this is Number Five—
Are you really still alive?
 Roll me over, lay me down, and do it again.
Now this is Number Six—
And I'm getting plenty kicks.
 Roll me over, lay me down, and do it again.

Roll Me Over in the Clover

Now this is Number Seven—
And for me it's just pure heaven!
    Roll me over, lay me down, and do it again.
Now this is Number Eight—
And the bastard's just dead weight!
    Roll me over, lay me down, and do it again.

Now this is Number Nine—
And your dong is in just fine!
    Roll me over, lay me down, and do it again.
Now this is Number Ten—
And I've worn out four big men!
    Roll me over, lay me down, and do it again.

Don't Call Me!

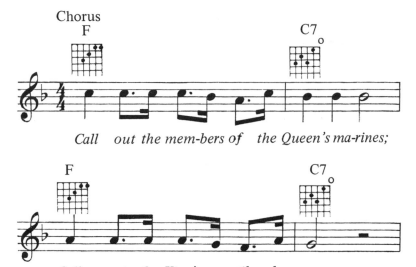

Chorus

Call   out the mem-bers of   the Queen's ma-rines;

Call   out   the King's ar - til - le - ry;

Call out my moth-er, my sis-ter, and my bro-ther, But for

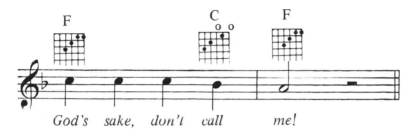

God's sake, sake, don't call me!

Verse

I___ don't want to be a sol - dier; I

don't want to be a man of Mars; I just want to go,

Don't Call Me!

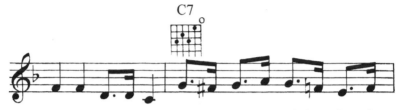

down to old So-ho, Pinch-in' all the girl-ies in the

shoul-der blades.__ I don't need no for-eign wom-en; Why

Lon-don's full of girls I've nev - er had. I

Don't Call Me!

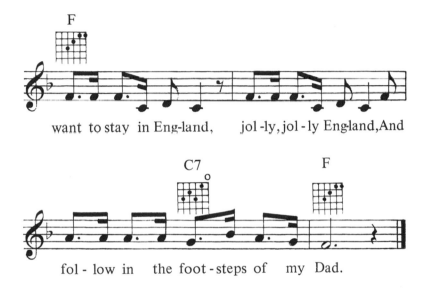

want to stay in Eng-land,   jol -ly, jol - ly England, And

fol - low in   the foot - steps of   my Dad.

CHORUS

Call out the members of the Queen's marines;
Call out the King's artillery;
Call out my mother, my sister, and my brother,
But for God's sake, don't call me!

Don't Call Me!

I don't want to be a soldier;
>   I don't want to be a man of Mars;
I just want to go,down to old Soho
>   Pinchin' all the girlies in the shoulder blades.
I don't need no foreign women;
>   Why London's full of girls I've never had.
I want to stay in England, jolly, jolly England,
>   And follow in the footsteps of my Dad.

Now Monday night my hand was on her ankle;
>   On Tuesday night my hand was on her knees;
Wednesday night—success! I lifted up her dress;
>   Thursday night I lifted up her silk chemise.
Friday night I got my hand upon it;
>   Saturday night I gave it just a tweak;
Sunday after supper, I finally got it up 'er,
>   And now I'm paying seven bob a week.

Don't Call Me!

Now I don't want to join the Navy;
    I don't want to go to war.
I want to hang around like a well-fed Beagle hound,
    Livin' off the riches of a wealthy lady.
I don't want a bullet in my backside;
    I don't want my knuckles shot away;
I want to stay in England, jolly, jolly England,
    And fornicate my bloomin' life away.

Saturday Night

Well, it was Sat - ur - day night, and

I came home As drunk as I could be;— And

there was this horse in the sta-ble Where

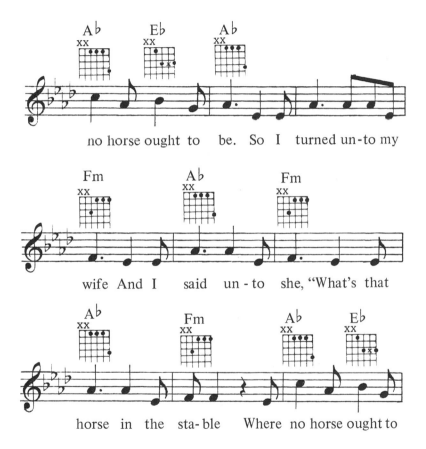

no horse ought to be. So I turned un-to my

wife And I said un - to she, "What's that

horse in the sta - ble Where no horse ought to

Saturday Night

Saturday Night

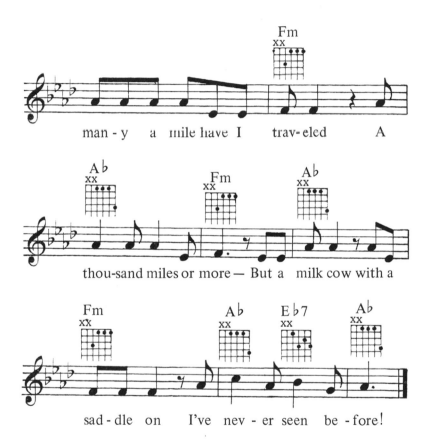

man - y   a   mile have I   trav- eled   A
thou-sand miles or more — But a   milk cow with a
sad - dle   on   I've   nev - er seen   be -fore!

Saturday Night

Well, it was Saturday night, and I came home
    As drunk as I could be;
And there was this horse in the stable
    Where no horse ought to be.
So I turned unto my wife
    And I said unto she,
"What's that horse in the stable
    Where no horse ought to be?"

    "Oh, you blind fool, you stupid fool,
        You fool, why can't you see?
    It's nothing but a milk cow
        My mother sent to me."

Oh, many a mile have I traveled—
    A thousand miles or more—
But a milk cow with a saddle on
    I've never seen before!

Saturday Night

Well, it was Saturday night, and I came home
    As busy as a bee;
And there was this coat on the hatrack
    Where no coat ought to be.
So I turned unto my wife
    And I said unto she,
"What's that coat on the hatrack
    Where no coat ought to be?"

    "Oh, you blind fool, you stupid fool,
        You fool, why can't you see?
    It's nothing but a blanket of mine
        My mother sent to me."

Oh, many a mile have I traveled—
    A thousand miles or more—
But a blanket with blue buttons on
    I've never seen before!

Saturday Night

Well, it was Saturday night, and I came home
    As charming as could be;
And there was this hat in the closet
    Where no hat ought to be.
So I turned unto my wife
    And I said unto she,
"What's that hat in the closet
    Where no hat ought to be?"

    "Oh, you blind fool, you stupid fool,
        You fool, why can't you see?
    It's nothing but a chamber pot
        My mother sent to me."

Oh, many a mile have I traveled—
    A thousand miles or more—
But a chamber pot with a hatband on
    I've never seen before!

Saturday Night

Well, it was Saturday night, and I came home
    As jolly as could be;
And there was this head on the pillow
    Where no head ought to be.
So I turned unto my wife
    And I said unto she,
"What's that head on the pillow
    Where no head ought to be?"

    "Oh, you blind fool, you stupid fool,
      You fool, why can't you see?
    It's nothing but a baby
      My mother sent to me."

Oh, many a mile have I traveled—
    A thousand miles or more—
But a baby with a moustache on
    I've never seen before!

The Princess Pappulie

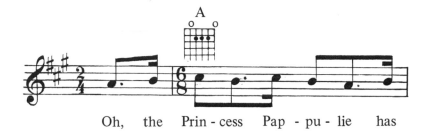

Oh, the Prin - cess Pap - pu - lie has

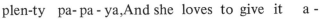

plen-ty pa-pa-ya, And she loves to give it a -

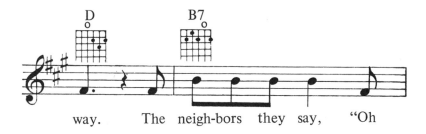

way. The neigh-bors they say, "Oh

me -ya! Oh my-ya!"You real - ly must try 'er! A

piece of the Prin - cess   Pa - pul-ie's pa-pa - ya!

Da - da - da - da - da - da - da - da - da!

The Princess Pappulie

One day it was Feel-Day in the groves of papaya;
    The customers came all day.
I came to the gate, and I felt hearty,
But I was tardy,
So I missed out on the Princess' big party!
    Da-da-da-da-da-da-da-da-da!

So let this be a warnin', go early in the mornin'
    And you'll never rue the day—
'Cause the Princess Pappulie has plenty papaya,
And she loves to give it away. I'm not a liar.
She loves to give it away. Just try 'er!
    Da-da-da-da-da-da-da-da-da!

The Princess Pappulie

Oh, the Princess Pappulie has plenty papaya,
    And she loves to give it away.
The neighbors they say, "Oh me-ya! Oh my-ya!"
You really must try 'er!
A piece of the Princess Pappulie's papaya!
    Da-da-da-da-da-da-da-da-da!

Oh, the Princess Pappulie is truly unruly,
    To handle papaya that way.
It seems to suit 'er, to give the fruit-a
But not the root-a,
So she has the fruit and the root to boot-a!
    Da-da-da-da-da-da-da-da-da!

The Amsterdam Maid

In Am-ster-dam I met a maid, Mark well what I do say! In Am-ster-dam I met a maid And she was mis-tress

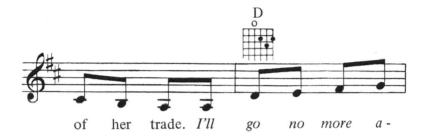

of her trade. *I'll go no more a -*

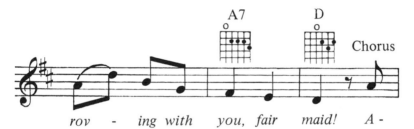

rov - ing with you, fair maid! A -

Chorus

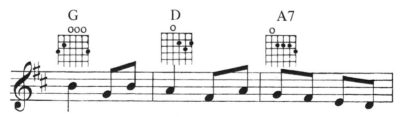

rov - ing, a - rov - ing, Since rov - ing's been my

The Amsterdam Maid

ru - i - en, I'll go no more a -

rov - ing with you, fair maid!

In Amsterdam I met a maid—
  Mark well what I do say!
In Amsterdam I met a maid
And she was mistress of her trade.
  I'll go no more a-roving with you, fair maid!

The Amsterdam Maid

CHORUS

A-roving, a-roving,
Since roving's been my ru-i-en,
I'll go no more a-roving with you, fair maid!

I put my arm around her waist—
    Mark well what I do say!
I put my arm around her waist;
Says she, "Young man, you're in great haste!"
    I'll go no more a-roving with you, fair maid!

I touched that fair maid on the toe;
Says she, "Young man, you're feelin' low!"

I touched that girl upon her knee;
Says she, "Young man, you're rather free!"

The Amsterdam Maid

I placed my hand upon her cunt;
She said, "Young man! That's an affront!"

I put my finger up her snatch;
"Good?" I asked, and she said, "Natch!"

I ran my cock right up her hole;
Said she, "You've got a mighty pole!"

I fucked her once; I fucked her twice;
"Young man," said she, "you're very nice."

I took my hat to say goodbye;
"Young man," said she, "you're very sly."

The Amsterdam Maid

I said, "What now, my pretty maid?"
She said, "You're fun—but I'll be paid!"

I said, "But you enjoyed it, too!"
"You bet!" said she. "As much as you!"

"Young man!" said she. "You're mighty brash!
I like it more when I get cash!"

A Squire of Great Renown

There was a squire of great re - nown, There

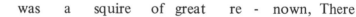

was a squire of great re - nown, There

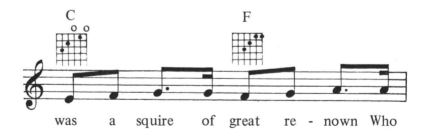

was a squire of great re - nown Who

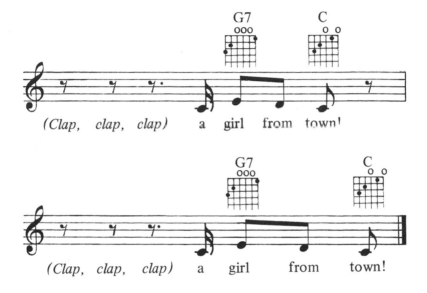

(Clap, clap, clap) a girl from town!

(Clap, clap, clap) a girl from town!

There was a squire of great renown,
There was a squire of great renown,
There was a squire of great renown
Who *(clap, clap, clap)* a girl from town.

A Squire of Great Renown

He met her first behind the mill,
And *(clap, clap, clap)* her up the hill.

He took her to his bachelor's bed,
And *(clap, clap, clap)* till she was dead.

And when the bells rang out "Amen,"
He *(clap, clap, clap)* her to life again.

And now the moral I will tell,
And now the moral I will tell—
If all the world seems false and fell
Just *(clap, clap, clap)* till all is well.

Oh, Dear! What Can the Matter Be?

Oh, dear! What can the mat-ter be?

Six old la-dies locked in a la-va-t'ry.

They were there from Sun-day to Sat-ur-day;

RIBALD SONGS

Oh, Dear! What Can the Matter Be?

No-bod-y   knew they were   there.___   The

first was the   Bi-shop of Chi-ches-ter's daugh-ter Who

went out   to   pass some su - per - flu - ous   wa-ter;She

Oh, Dear! What Can the Matter Be?

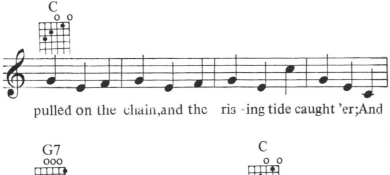

pulled on the chain, and the ris-ing tide caught 'er; And

no-bod-y   knew she was   there.____

Oh, dear! What can the matter be?
Six old ladies locked in a lavat'ry.
They were there from Sunday to Saturday;
 Nobody knew they were there!

Oh, Dear! What Can the Matter Be?

The first was the Bishop of Chichester's daughter
Who went out to pass some superfluous water;
She pulled on the chain, and the rising tide caught 'er;
   And nobody knew she was there.

The second was the stately Duchess of Roylett,
Who picked a poor time to go to the toilet;
We were having such fun—when she had to spoil it.
   And nobody knew she was there.

The third was the Abbess of Church Sweet Surrender
Who happened to loosen a nether suspender,
Which somehow got caught in her feminine gender;
   And nobody knew she was there.

Oh, Dear! What Can the Matter Be?

The fourth was the skinny Mary Maude Totham,
Her buttocks so scrawny—she tried to blot 'em,
And fell through the seat and plunged down to the bottom!
    And nobody knew she was there.

The fifth was the fidgety Georgina Treat;
Whose hair got caught in a cleft in the seat;
And the lady couldn't move not her ass nor her feet
    And nobody knew she was there.

The sixth was—Oh, pity!—an anonymous martyr
Who entered the privy to tighten a garter,
And was quite overcome by a high-powered farter;
    And nobody knew she was there.

Sweet Violets

My wife, she died in the

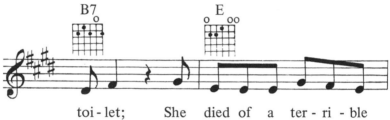

toi - let; She died of a ter - ri - ble

fit; To ful - fill her ver - y last

wish-es, She was bur-ied in six feet of

Sweet Vi-o-lets! Sweet-er than all the

ros-es. Cov-ered all o-ver from

Sweet Violets

head to toe, Cov-ered all o - ver with snow.

My wife she died in the toilet;
She died of a terrible fit;
To fulfill her very last wishes,
She was buried in six feet of ——

CHORUS

Sweet Violets!
Sweeter than all the roses.
Covered all over from head to toe,
Covered all over with snow.

Sweet Violets

My wife kept a sack in the garden;
    I was curious, I will admit.
One morning I sneaked out a handful
    And found it was nothing but ——

There was a young fellow from Sparta
    Who could flatulate ballads and airs.
He could blow out a Mozart sonata
    And accompany musical chairs.

One day he attempted an opera;
    It was hard, but he just wouldn't quit.
With his head held aloft, he suddenly coughed,
    And collapsed in a mountain of ——

Sweet Violets

I know that these verses are scanty;
    The rhyme seems too much for my wit.
I start out like Shakespeare and Dante;
    But somehow I wind up with ——

And now that my story has ended;
    And I must make my ex-IT;
If any of you feel offended,
    Stick your head in a barrel of ——

I sat on a gold lavatory
    In the home of the Baron of Split;
The seat was encrusted with rubies
    But, as usual, the bowl contained ——

The Wayward Boy

I walked the street with a tap to my feet; I
heard a voice a - bove me.   A   love-ly maid looked
down and said, "I   need some-one to   love me." Says

The Wayward Boy

I, "My dear, you need-n't fear, For I have heard your

plead - in'; You will find your joy with the

Way-ward Boy, He's got just what you're need-in'."

The Wayward Boy

I walked the street with a tap to my feet;
    I heard a voice above me.
A lovely maid looked down and said,
    "I need someone to love me."
Says I, "My dear, you needn't fear,
    For I have heard your pleadin';
You will find your joy with the Wayward Boy,
    He's got just what you're needin'."

"I've heard of you, my Wayward Boy,
    Your name is far exalted;
But I won't come down, I can't come down,
    My bedroom door is bolted.
My father is a minister,
    My maidenhead does cherish.
Nightly he does lock me in
    So lonely I do perish."

The Wayward Boy

Well, the fence was small; I shinnied up the wall;
    I stood there right behind her.
With quite some charm, she lifted up her arm
    And grabbed some clothes to hide her.
Says I, "Young maid, don't be afraid.
    Your future can be thrillin'.
If you're the one who likes a bit of fun,
    The Wayward Boy is willin.'"

Well, she jumped into bed and covered up her head,
    And she said I couldn't find her;
She knew damn well, she lied like hell—
    I jumped in right behind her.
I shoved my chest up to her breast;
    I shook her like a toy.
When I hit the bell, she knew damn well
    Why they call me the Wayward Boy.

The Wayward Boy

Well, the bed broke down, I landed on the ground.
    Her father come a-gunnin'.
I jumped through the glass, and landed on my ass—
    I got two feet a-runnin'.
Her father took aim through the windowpane,
    And a shotgun blasted by me.
And for weeks ahead, I was pickin' out the lead,
    With a mirror held behind me.

So the years went by. I woke up with a sigh
    As fancy did remind me.
And one fine day, I made my way
    To the gal I left behind me.
She still looked thin—to ward off sin—
    She didn't look much older;
But she had five girls and seven little boys
    And a baby on her shoulder.

The Chandler's Wife

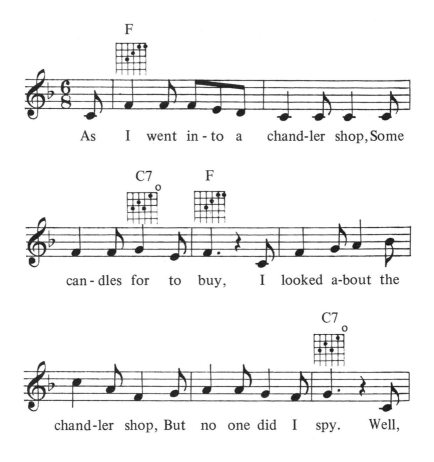

As I went in-to a chand-ler shop, Some
can-dles for to buy, I looked a-bout the
chand-ler shop, But no one did I spy. Well,

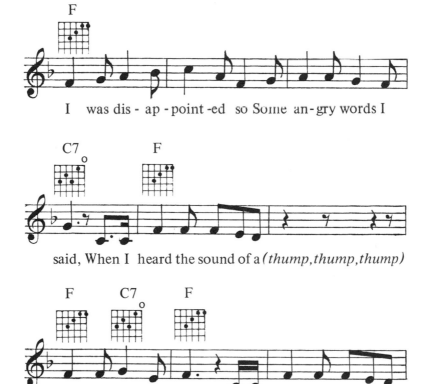

I   was dis - ap - point -ed so Some an-gry words I

said, When I heard the sound of a *(thump,thump,thump)*

Right a-bove my head. Yes,I heard the sound of the

The Chandler's Wife

(thump, thump, thump) Right a-bove my head.

As I went into a chandler shop,
    Some candles for to buy,
I looked about the chandler shop,
    But no one did I spy.
Well, I was disappointed so
    Some angry word I said,
When I heard the sound of a *(thump, thump, thump)*
    Right above my head.

The Chandler's Wife

Well, I was slick, and I was quick,
 So up the stairs I sped;
And very surprised was I to find
 The chandler's wife in bed.
And with her was another man
 Of quite considerable size;
And they were having a *(thump, thump, thump)*
 Right before my eyes.

And when the fun was over and done,
 The lady raised her head,
And very surprised, she said to me,
 As I stood by her bed,
"If you will be discreet, my boy,
 If you will be so kind,
You, too, can come up for some *(thump, thump, thump)*
 Whenever you feel inclined."

The Chandler's Wife

So, many a night and many a day,
    When the chandler wasn't home,
To get myself some candles
    To the chandler shop I'd roam.
But never a one she gave to me—
    She gave to me, instead,
Just a little more of that *(thump, thump, thump)*
    To light my way to bed.

Now all you married men take heed:
    Whenever you go to town,
If you must leave your woman alone,
    Be sure to tie her down.
Or if you would be kind to her,
    Just sit her down there on the floor
And give her so much of that *(thump, thump, thump)*
    That she won't want any more.

Rollin' Down the Mountain

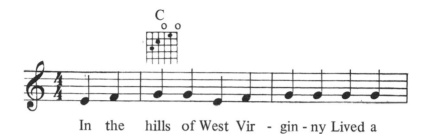

In the   hills of West Vir - gin - ny Lived a

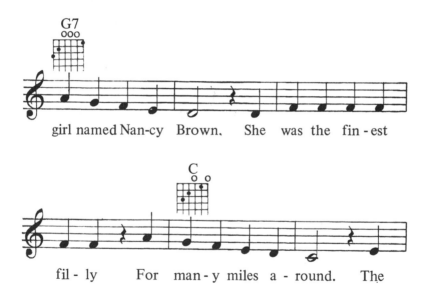

girl named Nan-cy Brown,   She   was the fin - est

fil - ly   For man - y miles a - round.   The

RIBALD SONGS

Rollin' Down the Mountain

dea - con came a - vis - it - in' From the

val - ley from be - low; He al - most reached the

sum - mit, But no fur - ther would she go.

Rollin' Down the Mountain

Chorus

And she came roll - in' down the moun-tain,

roll - in' down the moun-tain,   Roll-in' down the

moun-tain, shout-in' "No!"   And she did-n't give the

Rollin' Down the Mountain

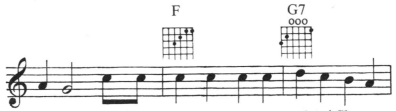

dea-con That there thing that he was seek-in', She re-

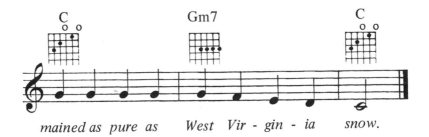

mained as pure as West Vir - gin - ia snow.

In the hills of West Virginny
　　Lived a girl named Nancy Brown.
She was the finest filly
　　For many miles around.

Rollin' Down the Mountain

The deacon came a-visitin'
　　From the valley from below;
He almost reached the summit—
　　But no further would she go.

And she came rollin' down the mountain,
　　Rollin' down the mountain,
　　She came rollin' down the mountain shoutin' "No!"
And she didn't give the deacon
That there thing that he was seekin'—
　　She remained as pure as West Virginia snow.

Well, along came a trapper ,
　　And he wooed her with a song;
He took her to the mountains,
　　But she still knew right from wrong.

Rollin' Down the Mountain

And she came rollin' down the mountain,
    Rollin' down the mountain,
    She came rollin' down the mountain breathin' storm.
And she left her bold companion
To the coyotes in the canyon.
    She remained as pure as West Virginia corn.

Well, along came a salesman
    With his phrases slick and kind;
Took Nancy up the mountain,
    But at last she read his mind.

And she came rollin' down the mountain,
    Rollin' down the mountain,
    She came rollin' down the mountain piggyback.
She remained as I have stated:
Not one wit contaminated.
    She remained as pure as pappy's applejack.

Rollin' Down the Mountain

Then along came a city slicker
    With his hundred dollar bills;
Took Nancy in his Cadillac,
    And kept her in the hills.

And so she stayed up in the mountain,
    Stayed up in the mountain,
    Oh, she stayed up in the mountain all that night.
She returned next morning early,
More a woman than a girlie;
    And her pappy kicked the hussy out of sight!

In a great big, fancy penthouse,
    Nancy Brown has got it made;
By the guy who keeps the penthouse,
    Nancy Brown is being laid.

Rollin' Down the Mountain

Now she's livin' in the city,
    Livin' in the city,
    Oh, she's livin' in the city mighty swell.
She is dancin', she is dinin';
On her fanny she's reclinin',
    And the West Virginia hills can go to hell!

The Jolly Tinker

There was a jol - ly tin - ker, and he came_ from_ France; There was a jol - ly tin - ker, and he came_ from_ France, With his

The Jolly Tinker

long - john— tid-dley-wack-er, fid-dley-wack-er

Chorus

pants. *With his long-john tid - dley wack - er,*

O - ver-grown kid-ney crack-er, Look-in' for a

The Jolly Tinker

cu - tie shack - er For to take him in.

There was a jolly tinker, and he came from France;
With his long-john tiddley-wacker, fiddley-wacker pants.

CHORUS

With his long-john tiddley-wacker,
Overgrown kidney cracker,
Lookin' for a cutie shacker
For to take him in.

The Jolly Tinker

Well, the farmer's daughter was a-comin' from the ball;
She met the jolly tinker; he was standin' by a wall.

She took one look and told him with a sigh,
"You're my darling, you're my dearest, you're the apple of my eye."

"Pretty maiden, pretty maiden, pretty maiden, I love you."
Said she, "My jolly tinker, just a half dollar'll do."

He took her by the hand for to bring her to the hay;
She got so eager, she dragged him all the way.

First he had her in the barn, then he had her in the hall;
The servants started screamin', "He's goin' to have us all!"

The Jolly Tinker

Well, when the fun was over, he shouldered up his load;
He brushed off his clothes and went whistlin' down the road.

"Oh, Mother!" cried the maiden, "I'm in trouble and alone,
For the tinker took his pleasure, and he's left me here to moan!"

"Daughter, you're a ninny, for you left it all to chance!
Don't give it to a tinker 'til he pays you in advance!"

Bible Stories

Come one, come all, come right a -

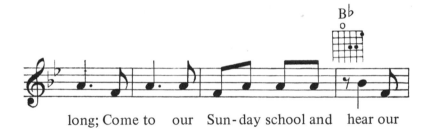

long; Come to our Sun-day school and hear our

song. Please to check your chew-ing gum and

ra - zors at the door, And you'll hear such Bi - ble

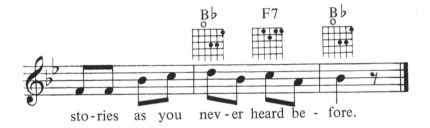

sto - ries as you nev - er heard be - fore.

Come one, come all, come right along;
Come to our Sunday school and hear our song.
Please to check your chewing gum and razors at the door,
And you'll hear such Bible stories as you never heard before

Bible Stories

Adam was the first man; Eve she was his wife;
They lived in the Garden, and they led a happy life.
But Eve ate of the apple, and so they couldn't remain,
So they moved into the suburbs, and they started raising Cain.

Adam had two sons who didn't quite agree;
The psychiatrists they conferred and said, " 'Twas sibling rivalry."
One day young Cain got angry, and somehow lost his head,
Took out his Colt revolver, and filled Abel full of lead.

The Lord created Satan, and Satan he made sin;
That's one time God came in leading with his chin.
For sin got so attractive, everbody joined the fun;
And now that all are sinning, the good Lord's work is done.

Bible Stories

Methuselah got real famous, for he refused to die;
"When ya gonna croak?" they asked. He answered, "Bye and bye."
And when they pressed him for the date, Methoozy whispered, "Hush!"
Then laughing through his whiskers, he hollered, "What's the rush?"

Noah was a sailor who built himself an ark;
And when the good Lord called a flood, old Noah did embark.
He took along the animals, and all the kiddies too;
And when the little ones were bored, he sent them to the zoo.

Onan, son of Judah, was a melancholy kid;
He'd jerk and jerk and jerk and jerk, and that was all he did.
But the Lord got very angry, when Onan shunned his mate;
So awfully hipped on self-abuse, he wouldn't fornicate.

Bible Stories

Joseph was a pretty boy, a very handsome kid;
His boss' wife she eyed him, and straight 'way flipped her lid.
She grabbed him by his you-know-what, and sat him on her lap;
But Joey wouldn't fall for that—he knew she had the clap.

Moses was a wise old bird who knew some fancy tricks;
The gyppos tried some phoney stuff, but Moe told off those pricks.
Old Pharoah did pursue him, and the Israelites did flee;
But Moses hexed those bastards, and he drowned them in the sea.

Joshua was a jazz cat—the greatest ever born;
The walls of Jericho fell down when he blew 'pon his horn.
Pursuing all his enemies, he bade the sun stand still;
The sun it wouldn't listen, so he nailed it to a hill.

Bible Stories

Samson was a strong boy who licked each kid in school;
Then Samson whipped the Philistines with the jawbone of a mule.
But along came Delilah, and acting on a hunch,
She shaved off Samson's whiskers, and the big boy lost his punch.

David was a shepherd lad—his mother's pride and joy;
He bought himself a slingshot—a harmless little toy.
Along came Goliath; "Go fuck you!" David said,
And heaving up a cobblestone, he crushed the giant's head.

Elijah was an astronaut—a very clever flyer;
He winged up to heaven in a chariot of fire.
But when he reached the pearly gates, the Lord began to frown;
"Now listen here, Elijah! Just haul those cinders down!"

Bible Stories

Jeremiah was a wailer who cried all night and day;
He balled and balled just bucketsful, and cried his eyes away.
They asked him, "What you cryin' for?" He grabbed a handkerchief—
"The worst, dear friends, has happened: my pecker won't get stiff!"

Jonah was a sailor; he went out for a sail;
He booked a steerage passage on a trans-Altantic whale.
He didn't like his quarters, although they were the best,
So he pushed a little button, and the whale it did the rest.

Daniel was saintly—the holiest of men;
The King got mad at Daniel and put him in a den.
Seemed Danny was a goner; they prepared a funeral wreath;
But Daniel was a dentist, and he pulled the lions' teeth.

Bible Stories

John was a Baptist whose look was hot as fire;
He took one look at Salome and filled her with desire.
She propositioned Johnny-boy who wouldn't get into bed,
So Johnny lost that piece of tail, and also lost his head.

Paul was a salesman who travelled far and wide;
But though he was a bachelor, he never went for hide.
He scorned every female, and preached that sex was out;
And 'twas all because Paul's peter was afflicted with the gout.

She Was Poor but She Was Honest

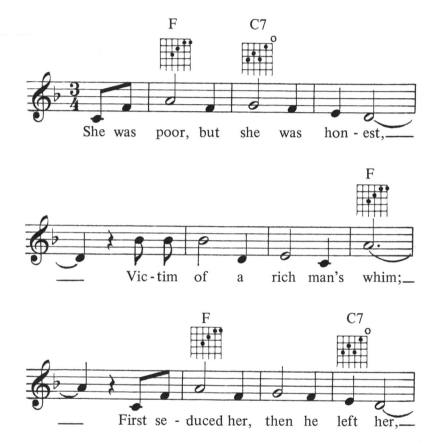

She was poor, but she was hon - est,___

___ Vic - tim of a rich man's whim;___

___ First se - duced her, then he left her,___

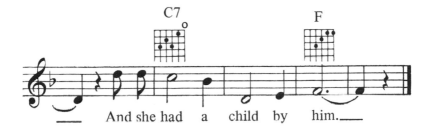

And she had a child by him.

She was poor but, she was honest,
    Victim of a rich man's whim;
First seduced her, then he left her,
    And she had a child by him.

CHORUS

> *It's the same the whole world over,*
>   *It's the poor what gets the blame;*
> *It's the rich gets all the pleasure,*
>   *Ain't it all a bleedin' shame!*

She Was Poor but She Was Honest

See him with his hounds and horses,
    See him strutting at his club;
While the victim of his whoring
    Drinks her gin inside a pub.

Then she came to London city
    Just to hide her bleeding shame;
But a Labour leader screwed her,
    Put her on the streets again!

See him in the House of Commons
    Passing laws to combat crime;
While the victim of his evil
    Walks the streets at night in shame.

She Was Poor but She Was Honest

See him riding in a carriage,
    Past the gutter where she stands;
He has made a stylish marriage
    While she wrings her ringless hands.

See her on the bridge at midnight
    Throwing snowballs at the moon;
She said, "Jack, I never 'ad it!"
    But she spoke too goddamn soon.

See her stand in Piccadilly
    Offering her aching quim;
She is now completely ruined
    And 'twas all because of him!

She Was Poor but She Was Honest

Now you'll find her in the theatre;
　See her sitting in the stalls;
She'll be home an hour later
　Playing with some stranger's balls.

See him passing in his carriage
　With his face all wreathed in smiles;
See her sitting on the pavement
　Which is bloody bad for piles.

Then there came a wealthy pimper,
　Marriage was the tale he told;
She had no one else to take her
　So she sold her soul for gold.

She Was Poor but She Was Honest

In a little country cottage
    There her grieving parents live;
Though they drink the fizz she sends them
    Yet they never will forgive.

See him seated in his Rolls Royce
    Driving homeward from the hunt;
He got riches from his marriage—
    She got corns upon her cunt.

Caviar

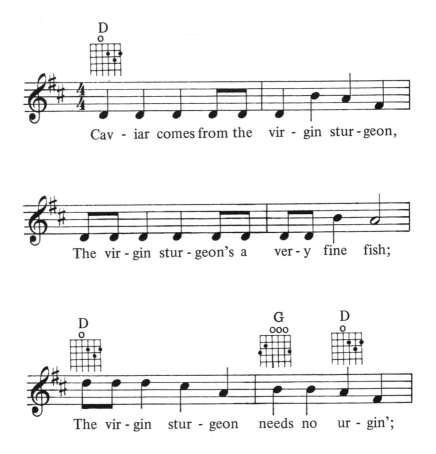

Cav - iar comes from the vir - gin stur - geon,

The vir - gin stur - geon's a ver - y fine fish;

The vir - gin stur - geon needs no ur - gin';

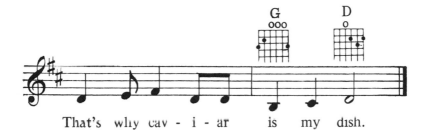

That's why cav - i - ar   is   my   dish.

Caviar comes from the virgin sturgeon,
    The virgin sturgeon's a very fine fish;
The virgin sturgeon needs no urgin'
    That's why caviar is my dish.

I gave caviar to my girl friend,
    She was a virgin tried and true;
Ever since she had the caviar,
    There ain't nothing she won't do!

RIBALD SONGS

Caviar

I gave caviar to my grandpa,
    Grandpa's age is ninety-three;
And next time I saw grandpa,
    He'd chased grandma up a tree.

Ivan Skavinsky Skavar

The har - ems of E - gypt are fine to be - hold; The fair - est of har - lots ap - pear; But the fair - est

RIBALD SONGS

Ivan Skavinsky Skavar

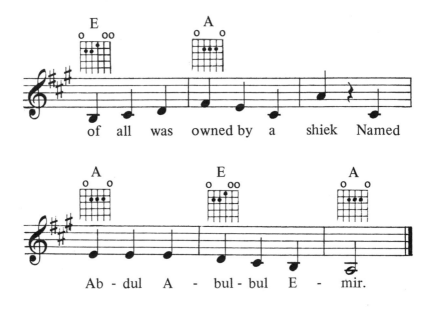

of all was owned by a shiek Named

Ab - dul A - bul - bul E - mir.

The harems of Egypt are fine to behold;
The fairest of harlots appear;
But the fairest of all was owned by a sheik
Named Abdul Abulbul Emir.

Ivan Skavinsky Skavar

A travelling brothel came down from the North
    Arrangements made just for the Tsar,
Who wagered a buck no one could outfuck
    Ivan Skavinsky Skavar.

A day was arranged for the spectacle great,
    A holiday set by the Tsar;
And the streets were all lined with the harlots assigned
    To Ivan Skavinsky Skavar.

Old Abdul came in with his dames by his side;
    His eye bore a leer of desire;
And he started to brag just how he'd surely outshag
    Ivan Skavinsky Skavar.

Ivan Skavinsky Skavar

All hairs they were shorn, no frenchies were worn,
    And this suited Abdul by far;
And he quite set his mind on a fast action grind
    To beat Ivan Skavinsky Skavar.

They met on the track with cocks at the slack,
    A starter's gun punctured the air;
They were both quick to rise. The crowd gaped at the size
    Of Abdul Abulbul Emir.

They worked all the night in the pale yellow light,
    Old Abdul he revved like a car;
But he couldn't compete with the slow steady beat
    Of Ivan Skavinsky Skavar.

Ivan Skavinsky Skavar

So Ivan he won. And he stooped for his gun;
    And he bent down, exploring his rear.
When something red hot, up his back passage shot—
    'Twas Abdul Abulbul Emir!

The harlots turned green! The crowd shouted "Quean!"
    They were ordered apart by the Tsar.
'Twas bloody bad luck, for poor Abdul was stuck
    Up Ivan Skavinsky Skavar.

The cream of the joke came when both of them broke—
    'Twas laughed at for years by the Tsar—
For Abdul, the fool, had left half his tool
    Up Ivan Skavinsky Skavar!

The Old Gray Bustle

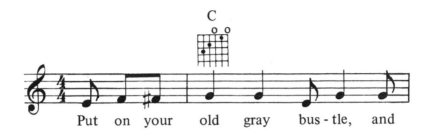

Put on your old gray bus - tle, and

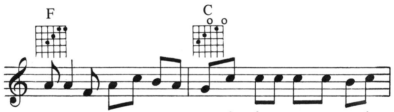

get out and hus-tle, For to-mor-row there's a mort-gage com-ing

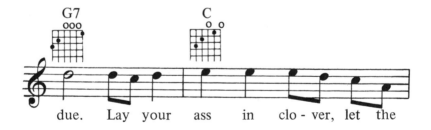

due. Lay your ass in clo - ver, let the

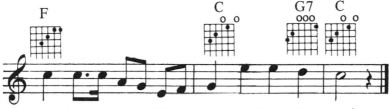

boys look it o-ver; If you can't get five, take two!

Put on your old gray bustle, and get out and hustle,
  For tomorrow there's a mortgage coming due.
Lay your ass in clover, let the boys look it over,
  If you can't get five, take two!

Put on the old blue ointment, the crabs' disappointment,
  And we'll kill the bastards where they lay.
It scratches and it itches; but 'twill kill the sons-of-bitches
  In the good old-fashioned way.

The Old Gray Bustle

Put on those old red panties that used to be your auntie's,
  And we'll have a little frolic in the hay;
And while they're out there hayin', we'll both be in here layin',
  In the good old-fashioned way.

We Go to College

We go to col - lege! We like to dance!

We don't wear bras, but we all wear pants. We

al - ways give the fresh - men a chance.

RIBALD SONGS

We Go to College

We are from Col - lege Hall.

We go to college! We like to dance!
We don't wear bras, but we wear zipped pants.
We always give the freshmen a chance.
We are from College Hall.

We go to college. Don't we have fun?
We know exactly how it is done.
We saw the movies in Hygiene A-1.
We are from College Hall.

We Go to College

We go to college. We can be had.
Don't take what we say—just ask your dad.
All his old buddies did sexual studies!
We are from College Hall.

We go to college. Don't we have pluck!
We don't like to work, but we like to fuck.
Come over, boys! And you may be in luck!
We are from College Hall.

Dicta

"This is going to run into money!" said the monkey as he pissed on the cash register.

※　※　※

"That remains to be seen!" said the elephant as he shit on the pavement.

※　※　※

Confusius say: Woman who cooks carrots and peas in same pot very unsanitary.

※　※　※

The newlyweds wanted to fly United, but the hostess objected.

※　※　※

She said she wanted a cocktail—so I told her one.

Catholic prayer: Oh, blessed Virgin, thou who didst conceive
without sinning, teach us to sin without conceiving.

※　　※　　※

A dog's idea of paradise: A thousand miles of telephone poles
and a belly full of piss.

※　　※　　※

Rape is impossible because a girl can run faster with her
skirt up than a man can with his pants down.

※　　※　　※

Never make love on an empty stomach. Feed her first.

※　　※　　※

Did you hear about the ruptured Chinaman? He was called
Wun Hong Lo.

If all the freshmen up at Yale were laid end to end—
I wouldn't be surprised.

❉   ❉   ❉

Did you hear about the queer parrot? He went for a cockatoo.

❉   ❉   ❉

Did you hear about the queer sparrow? He went for a
woodpecker.

❉   ❉   ❉

Did you hear about the two queer judges who
tried each other?

❉   ❉   ❉

The priest of my church loves his neighbor—but her
husband keeps showing up at the wrong time.

The best way to make a bull sweat is to give him a tight
    jersey.

❊   ❊   ❊

Fighting for peace is like fucking for chastity.

❊   ❊   ❊

Ever hear about the "Tight-skinned Giraffe?" Every time
    he winks his eye he dislocates his asshole.

❊   ❊   ❊

Zoroaster. And she said yes.

❊   ❊   ❊

He didn't believe in flying saucers —until he goosed
    the waitress.

Quatrains

The Proprieties Observed

The dean undressed with pious zest,
　　The vicar's wife to lie on;
She thought it rude to do it nude—
　　So he kept his old school tie on.

Baffling

Oysters are prolific bivalves,
　　Rear their young ones in their shell;
How they piddle is a riddle,
　　But they do, so what the hell!

Ecstasy

I love her in her evening gown;
I love her in her nightie;
    But when moonlight flits between her tits—
Jesus Christ Almighty!

Bride's Soliloquy

The cold cream is on the mantel,
    The shoe horn is on the shelf.
I saw that great big thing of yours —
    And I chloroformed myself.

Voice from the Pulpit

Down in the belfry a chauffeur lies,
The vicar's wife between his thighs.
Voice from the pulpit comes from afar:
"Stop fuckin' my wife, and start the car!"

Eyes of Brown

Here's to the girl with eyes of brown,
Who makes her living upside down;
Fifteen cents is the regular price—
Give her a quarter—she'll do it twice.

Here's to the Bull

Here's to the bull that roams the wood;
He does the cows and heifers good;
And if 'twere not for his long, long rod,
We'd not have any beef, by God!

Drifting

Drifting down the stream of Izzen,
    They were seated in the stern;
And she had her hand on hizzen,
    And he had his hand on hern.

Keep Off

If I had a girl and she was mine,
I'd paint her tits with iodine;
And on her belly I'd paint a sign:
"Keep off the grass! This ass is mine."

The Queen of Spain

"It's a helluva life!" said the Queen of Spain;
"Five months' pleasure and nine months' pain.
Four weeks' rest, and at it again;
It's a helluva life!" said the Queen of Spain.

Epitaph

Here lies the body of my daughter Charlotte,
Born a virgin and died a harlot.
For twelve long years she kept her virginity,
Which is quite a record for this vicinity.

Here's to the Split

Here's to the split that never heals;
The longer you rub it the better it feels.
And all the soap this side of hell
Can't wash away that fishy smell.

No Excuse

There are so many feather beds,
So many little maidenheads,
There's practically no excuse
For sodomy or self-abuse.

Know-How

The rich man uses vaseline,
    The poor man uses lard;
The worker uses axle grease
    But gets it twice as hard.

Lament

"If the skirts get any shorter,"
      Said the flapper with a sob,
"I'll have two more cheeks to powder
      And a lot more hair to bob."

Shock

I crept upstairs, my shoes in hand,
      Just as the night took wing,
And saw my wife, four steps above,
      Doing the same darned thing!

A Fool There Was

A fool there was, and he made his prayer
To a rag, a bone, and a hank of hair;
He placed his bone in the hank o' hair,
But the fool was fooled—the rag was there!

Fanny Hicks

Here lies the amorous Fanny Hicks,
The scabbard of ten thousand pricks;
And if you wish to do her honor —
Pull out your cock, jerk off upon her.

Man on Top of Woman

Man on top of woman, hasn't long to stay,
His head is full of business, and his ass is full of play;
He goes in like a lion, and he comes out like a lamb;
He buttons up his pants, and he doesn't give a damn!

Misled

Little Mary pinned her hopes
On a book by Mary Stopes;
Judging by the girl's condition,
It must have been an old edition.

Ah! Woe!

Your spooning days are over,
    And your pilot light is out;
When what used to be your sex appeal
    Is now your water spout!

Compensation

I've got an Aunt Kitty
Who has only one titty;
But it's long and it's pointed
And the nipple's double-jointed.

In Days of Old

In days of old when knights were bold
And women weren't particular;
They lined them up against the wall
And fucked them perpendicular.

Pretty Neat

In days of old when knights were bold
And paper not invented;
They wiped their ass with tufts of grass,
And they were quite contented.

Foolhardy

Little Mary took her skates
Upon the ice to frisk;
Wasn't she a little fool
Her little *

Plea

Oh, my darling, don't say no!
On the sofa you must go!
Petticoat up, and down with drawers!
You tickle mine and I'll tickle yours.

Nice Trick

You can talk about fucking; well, fucking's all right.
I fucked with a whore twenty times in one night,
And each time I fucked her, I came out a quart.
If you don't think that's fucking, well, you fucking well ort.

A Push in the Bush

Here's to America, land of the push,
Where a bird in the hand is worth two in the bush,
But if in the bush a fair maiden should stand,
Then a push in the bush is worth two in the hand.

Graffiti

Do something big—fuck a gaint.

❉　　❉　　❉

Preserve wildlife—throw a party.

❉　　❉　　❉

Uptight? Sex is great when you're up tight.

❉　　❉　　❉

Meet me in front of the pawnshop, and I'll kiss you
    under the balls!

❉　　❉　　❉

Avoid the draft—zip up your fly.

❉　　❉　　❉

Bucks with short horns should stand close.

❉　　❉　　❉

Stop screwing around—patronize your local brothel!

Don't piss on the floor—the next man may have holes
    in his shoes.

❋   ❋   ❋

You can shake it and shake it as long as you please;
But the last drop will always drip down to your knees.

❋   ❋   ❋

(On inside wall of pay toilet) SMILE, PLEASE! YOU ARE
ON TV.

❋   ❋   ❋

    A man must have no pride at all,
    If he writes his name on a shithouse wall.

❋   ❋   ❋

        If I should die in Tennessee,
        Who'll say *kadish* over me?

GRAFFITI

VERSE

Those Four-Letter Words

Banish the use of the four-letter words
    Whose meanings are never obscure.
The Angles and Saxons, those bawdy old birds,
    Were vulgar, obscene, and impure.
But cherish the use of the weak-kneed phrase
    That never quite says what you mean;
Far better you stick to your hypocrite ways
    Than be vulgar, coarse, or obscene.

When Nature is calling, plain speaking is out,
When ladies, God bless 'em, are milling about,
You *make water, wee-wee,* or *empty the glass;*
You can *powder your nose;* "*Excuse me*" may pass;
Shake the dew off the lily; see a man 'bout a dog;
Or when everyone's soused, it's *condensing the fog.*
But be pleased to consider and remember just this—
That only in Shakespeare do characters piss!

You may speak of a movement or sit on a seat,
Have a passage, or stool, or simply excrete;
Or say to the others, *I'm going out back,*
Then groan in pure joy in that smelly old shack.
You can go *lay a cable,* or do *number two*
Or sit on the toidey and make a *do-do,*
But ladies and men who are socially fit
Under no provocation will go take a shit!

When your dinners are hearty with onions and beans,
With garlic and claret and bacon and greens;
Your bowels get so busy distilling a gas
That Nature insists you permit it to pass.
You are very polite, and you try to exhale
Without noise or odor—you frequently fail—
Expecting a zephyr, you carefully start,
But even a deaf one would call it a fart!

Those Four-Letter Words

A woman has bosoms, a bust, or a breast,
Those lily-white swellings that bulge 'neath her vest;
They are towers of ivory, sheaves of new wheat;
In a moment of passion, ripe apples to eat.
You may speak of her nipples as small rings of fire
With hardly a question of raising her ire;
But by Rabelais' beard, she'll throw fifteen fits
If you speak of them roundly as good honest tits!

It's a cavern of joy you are thinking of now,
A warm, tender field just waiting the plow.
It's a quivering pigeon caressing your hand,
Or that sweet little pussy that makes a man stand.
Or perhaps it's a flower, a grotto, a well,
The hope of the world, or a velvety hell.
But, friend, heed this warning, beware the affront
Of aping a Saxon: don't call it a cunt!

Those Four-Letter Words

Though a lady repel your advance, she'll be kind
Just as long as you intimate what's on your mind.
You may tell her you're hungry, you *need to be swung*,
You may ask her to see how your etchings are hung.
You may mention the *ashes that need to be hauled;*
Put the lid on her sauce-pan, but don't be too bald;
For the moment you're forthright, get ready to duck—
The girl isn't born yet who'll stand for "Let's fuck!"

Banish the use of the four-letter words
      Whose meanings are never obscure.
The Angles and Saxons, those bawdy old birds,
      Were vulgar, obscene, and impure.
But cherish the use of the weak-kneed phrase
      That never quite says what you mean;
Far better you stick to your hypocrite ways
      Than be vulgar, coarse, or obscene.

The Family Tart

It fairly broke the family's heart
When Lady Jane became a tart;
But blood is blood and race is race,
And so to save the family face,
They bought her an expensive flat
With *Welcome* written on the mat.

It was not long ere Lady Jane
Brought her noble charms to fame;
A clientele of sahibs pukka
Came to London just to fuck 'er!
And it was whispered without malice
She had one client from the palace.

No one could nestle in her charms
Unless he wore ancestral arms;
No one inside her could gain entry
Unless he were of landed gentry;
In time that charming feline pet
Had screwed 'bout half the upper set.

When Lady Anne became a whore
It grieved the family even more;
They felt they ought to do the same
As they had done for Lady Jane;
They bought her an exclusive beat,
On expensive Jermyn Street.

The Family Tart

When Lord St. Clancy became a nancy
It did not please the family fancy;
And so in order to protect him
They did tattoo upon his rectum:
"All commoners avoid the steerage—
This fuckin' hole's reserved for peerage!"

The Camel

The sex life of the camel
    Is not as dull as one thinks;
In moments of animal passion
    He makes crude attempts at the Sphinx.

But the Sphinx's posterior passage
    Is clogged with the sands of the Nile,
Which accounts for the hump on the camel,
    And the Sphinx's inscrutable smile.

John the Baptist

John the Baptist was a saint;
Salome, a queen.
One wore haloes, one wore paint;
Both inhabited a dream.
Now John was quite a happy fellow
'Til the day when he did bellow,
"Paint and haloes cannot mix!"
Poor John-the-B was in a fix.
Salome just rolled her eyes;
She wanted John between her thighs.
She showed her breasts; she dropped her veils;
But John was adamant as nails.
So Salome, that sensual fish,
She took an ax and brought a dish
And put John's head upon the block.
John lost his head, but saved his cock.

He went to Heaven, minus head,
While Salome just went to bed.

The moral of this tale, it seems,
Is better learn to mix your dreams.

Edith Donahue McQuellan

Edith Donahue McQuellan
Ate her fill of watermelon.
Late that night with Richard Pruitt
Edith wet before she knew it.

Girls who can't control the bladder
Ne'er will top the social ladder.

Dear Old Greenwich Village

Down in dear old Greenwich Village,
Where they sport all sorts of frillage,
Where the spinsters hie for thrillage,
    Here's all kinds of crazy.
Down around dear old Eighth Street,
Which the Buddhists turned to "Faith Street,"
Beats and kooks stroll on this wraith street,
    Acting somewhat lazy.

Down in dear old Greenwich Village,
Which consumes so much distillage,
Where good manners are just nillage,
    Seek not peace nor quiet.
Freaks pour in from subway station,
Freaks from every clime and nation,
Come with lurid expectation
    Of a jolly riot.

Dear Old Greenwich Village

Here all movies are symbolic;
Here all infants have the colic;
Here the hippies strut and rolic
    Beggin' for a quarter.
Houses have such quaint old shutters;
Dog-shit lines the curbs and gutters;
Demonstrations front of Sutter's
    Might include your daughter.

Village! Hah! So unbucolic!
Gay boys cluster here to frolic
Midst the barflies melancholic
    On a liquid diet.
Hop-heads crowd in by the dozens,
Speed and smack and all their cousins;
Breezes carry all the buzzin's
    Where a head can buy it.

Dear Old Greenwich Village

If you seek the pornographic,
Are enthralled by ethnographic,
Just follow, please, the heavy traffic
    Past the Women's Prison.
Here the fashion illustrators,
And the high-priced decorators,
Have become just fornicators,
    Each a-seekin' his'n.

Scene of so much petty pillage!
Here's to dear old Greenwich Village!
Mecca of the neighboring swillage
    From Bensonhurst and Rego.
If you are a high-class fuck-up,
And you deem yourself unstuck-up,
The Village is the place to buck up
    Your declining ego.

Bridget O'Flaherty McHugh

Bridget O'Flaherty McHugh
Held venal traffic with a gnu.
    Mistaking fore for aft one morn
    Impaled herself upon its horn.
        Moral: Those who seek high ends
        Should shun our furred and feathered friends.

Cedric Tillinghast O'Brien

    Cedric Tillinghast O'Brien
    Tried to masturbate a lion.
        Playing with its lordly jock
        He was ripped from nape to nock.
            Moral: Those who play with Leo,
            Gloria in excelsis Deo!

Sonia Snell

This is the tale of Sonia Snell
To whom an accident befell;
An accident, as will be seen,
Embarrassing in the extreme.
It happened as it does to many
That Sonia went to spend a penny;
And entering with unconscious grace
The properly appointed place,
There behind the railway station
She sat in silent meditation . . .

Unfortunately, unacquainted,
The seat had recently been painted.
Too late did Sonia realize
Her inability to rise;

Sonia Snell

And though she struggled, pulled and yelled,
She found that she was firmly held.
She raised her voice in mournful shout,
"Please, someone, come and get me out."
A crowd stood 'round and feebly sniggered,
A signalman said, "I'll be jiggered."
"Gor blimey!" said an ancient porter,
"We ought to soak her orf wiv water!"
The station master and his staff
Were most polite and did not laugh.
They tugged at Sonia's hands and feet
But could not shift her off the seat.

A carpenter arrived at last
And finding Sonia still stuck fast,
Remarked, "I know what I can do."
And quickly sawed the seat in two!

Sonia Snell

Sonia arose, only to find
A wooden halo on her behind!
An ambulance drove down the street
And bore her off—complete with seat.
They rushed the wooden-bustled girl
Quickly to the hospital;
And grasping her by hands and head
Placed her downwards on a bed.
The doctors came and cast their eyes
Upon the seat with some surprise.
A surgeon said, "Now mark my word
Could anything be more absurd?
Has anyone, I implore,
Seen anything like this before?"

"Yes," cried a student, unashamed,
"Frequently—but never framed!"

That Short Word

Those portions of a woman that appeal to man's depravity
   Are fashioned with extraordinary care;
And what often seems to us to be a simple little cavity,
   Is really an elaborate affair.

There's the vulva, the vagina, and the jolly perineum,
   The hymen, which is sometimes found in brides,
And lots of other fancy names that I just cannot remember,
   The clitoris—and Christ knows what besides!

Now doctors of distinction have examined these phenomena
   In dozens of experimental dames;
And made a list of all the things in feminine abdomina,
   And given them delightful Latin names.

So isn't it a pity when we common people chatter
    Of the mysteries to which I have referred,
That we use for such a delicate and complicated matter,
    Such a short and very unattractive word!

Parodies

The Raving

Once upon a midnight dreary,
While I pondered weak and weary,
    And my ass was slowly draggin',
        My poor feet across the floor;
Suddenly, I heard a rapping—
"'Tis some little cutie tapping,
        Tapping at my hotel door.
'Tis some chippy that's a-wishin'
To my room to gain admission—
I could use a quick emission,
        Even though she be a whore."
        Said I tartly—"So I'll bore."

Open wide I flung the portal—
And before me stood a mortal
        As in all my living moments
            I had never seen before!
None had she of upper garments;
And of all seductive varmints,
        She was sure the warmest baby
            That these eyes had ever saw!
            Lord of Mercy! Give me more!

And each palpitating bubby
Was so round and firm and chubby,
        That my spirit rose within me.
            Spirit said I?—Something more!
Truth to speak—and it bears mention—
I felt such a grave distention
That I scarce could bear the tension,
            As it seemed to reach the floor!
            What a hard-on! I could roar!

The Raving

How can I describe the feeling,
As my ass near hit the ceiling;
    For I screwed that lovely pussy,
        Drove it almost through the floor!
And she lay there, pantin', writhin',
Twined around me like a python,
As I drove my swollen scythe in;
        Fucked that angel two times more.
        I could come forevermore!

'Twas the fourteenth of December,
'Twas a day I must remember—
    But my mem'ry veers more strongly
        To the day, December four.
Ten days past, I'd banged that siren,
With my big-deal shootin' iron.
I woke up to find poor Myron
        Bought himself a real *what-for!*
        Oh, VD is such a bore!

The Raving

Now I know what passed between us:
As I gaze on my poor penis,
　　Drooping, red, and penitential
　　　　And excruciating sore.
And weak tea is all I'm sipping;
And that cock of mine's still dripping,
　　Every morn, and every evening,
　　　　Dripping on the bathroom floor!
　　May *she* drip for evermore!

Oh, that dame won't be forgotten;
For each time I change the cotton,
　　I hear that chippy, rapping, tapping
　　　　Tapping at my chamber door.
Weakly do I make my answer:
"Are you peddlin' lice or cancer?
　　Take away your goddamned pussy,
　　　　Pussy with its charms galore!
　　I am groaning, '*Nevermore!*'"

Bye, Bye, Blackbird

Back your ass against the wall,
Here I come, balls and all—
>   Bye, bye cherry!
I ain't got a helluva lot,
But what I got will fill your twat.
>   Bye, bye, cherry!
You took me to your hut into the wildwood,
And there you took advantage of my childhood.
Hoist your ass and shake a tit,
Guide my prick into your slit.
>   Cherry! Bye, bye!

SHE:

Take off all your underwear,
I don't care if you're bare.
    Bye, bye, blackbird.
You taught me how to dance and sing
And even how to shake that thing.
    Bye, bye, blackbird.
You took me to your hut into the wildwood,
And there you took advantage of my childhood.
Put your hand beneath my dress,
And here you'll find a blackbird's nest—
    Boy friend! Bye, bye!

After Tennyson

Home they brought her warrior, fed
    To repletion more than just;
And the servants, chuckling, said,
    "He must shit, or he will bust."

Then they gave him castor oil,
    Pills and drugs of many a sort;
Yet despite their loving toil,
    He would not be taken short.

Stole a maiden to the spot,
    And cajoling, laughing, dared;
Yet in vain she held the pot,
    For he only belched and glared.

Came a nurse of ninety years,
    And a clyster huge she bore;
Shoved it up his ass—wild cheers!
    As he shat forevermore!

Tramp, Tramp, Tramp

He was sitting in the prison with his head between his hands,
And the shadow of his prick against the wall,
And the hairs grew thick from his knees up to his prick,
And the rats were playing billiards with his balls.

Dangerous Dan McGrew

His shirt was split, and caked with shit,
    And he sat down on a keg;
And we all could see, he had to pee,
    As the piss rolled down his leg.
Then "Boys!" said he, "You don't know me,
    And I don't give a fuck—
But there's one man here I'd drown in beer—
    If its froth was shit and muck!"

"He took my broad! He did, by Gawd!
    He stole that gal called Lou!
He's a bloody punk and a stinkin' skunk,
    And I mean Dan McGrew!"
Then the lights went out, and we hit the floor,
    And we huddled in the dark;
And the stranger drew, and the sparks they flew,
    And his bullet found its mark.

A bunch of the boys were whoopin' it up
    In one of the Yukon halls;
The kid that handled the music box
    Just sat a-scratchin' his balls.
The faro guy was making a try
    For the lady known as Lou;
And there on the floor, on top of a whore,
    Lay Dangerous Dan McGrew.

Then out of the night that was black as a bitch,
    And into the mob and the glare,
Strode a musty prick, just in from the crick,
    With the look of a titless mare.
Then he shouldered his way through that human decay,
    As he clutched at the crotch of his pants;
And he looked like a sap with a ripe dose of clap
    Plus a touch of Saint Vitus Dance.

Dangerous Dan McGrew

Then the lights went up, and that sickly pup
    Now grinned with the grin of Pan;
For there on the floor, with his asshole tore,
    Lay that no-good Dangerous Dan.
And the stranger beamed, and he looked, it seemed,
    Like he'd been born anew——
For perched on his pole was the lovely hole
    Of the lady that's known as Lou.

The Walrus and the Carpenter

"If all the whores with dirty drawers
    Were lying in the Strand;
Do you suppose," the Walrus said,
    "That we could raise a stand?"
"I doubt it," said the Carpenter,
    "But wouldn't it be grand?"
And all the while the dirty sod
    Was coming in his hand.

Anniversary Waltz

Oh, how we danced on the night we were wed;
We danced and we danced 'cause the room had no bed!

The Old Broken Fuckit

How dear to my heart was the old-fashioned harlot
    When fond recollection presents her to view;
The madam who bought her beer by the carlot,
    And offered the gentry an old-fashioned screw.
You may talk, if you will, of those cool innovations
    Imported from France which they nowadays tout;
But give me the natural, carnal sensations
    Of the old-fashioned harlot with her direct route.

How dear to my heart was the old-fashioned harlot
    Whose regular price was five dollars a leap;
I was really quite fond of those women in scarlet
    With whom I was wont, on occasion, to sleep.
You may sing or may trumpet the old-fashioned bucket
    That idyllically swung in a moss-girdled well;
But give me a strumpet who just wants to fuck it
    And gives you a workout that makes you feel swell.

My Secret Love

Once I had a secret love,
That lived within the heart of me.
When I asked my love about her fee,
She said for me the fee was free.
When I asked why it was free,
She said, "Seeley Mattress sponsors me!
Last night, we were on Channel Four!"
Now my secret love's no secret anymore!

Old Smokey

On top of old Rachel, all covered with sweat,
I've been fucking two hours, and I haven't come yet.

Sweet Alice

Oh, do you remember sweet Alice, Ben Bolt,
    Sweet Alice with cunt soft and brown;
How she'd grin with delight when you shoved in your dick
    And quickly she'd fetch your stiff prick down.

The poor girl is now so much older, Ben Bolt,
    And that soft, luscious pussy's now dry;
You couldn't edge in with a crowbar, Ben Bolt;
    The hole thing could make you sit and cry!

The Burial of Sir John Thomas

Not a sound was heard, but the ottoman shook,
    And my darling looked awfully worried;
As 'round her fair body a firm hold I took,
    And John Thomas I silently buried.

We buried him deeply at dead of night,
    The tails of our nightshirts upturning;
With struggling raptures and fits of delight,
    And the night lights dimly burning.

No horrible sheaths enclosed his crest,
    Not in rubber nor plastic we bound him;
But he went like a warrior taking his rest,
    With naught but a halo around him.

Few and short were the sighs we gave,
    Though we oftentimes groaned as in sorrow;
As at each joyous stroke, in rapture we'd rave,
    With scarce a thought for the morrow.

When John Thomas came out of his warm, narrow bed,
    As droopy as any sad willow;
How lowly hung down his now lifeless head!
    How gladly he'd rest on his pillow!

Be It Ever So Humble

Mid pleasures and palaces and 'specially when alone,
Be it ever so humble, there's no cock like your own!
It may dingle and dangle and fail to go to bone;
But how ever disabled, there's no dick like your own.

You stand in the Men's Room, the next guy's six foot tall;
Compared to his pecker, your thing is awfully small.
Your dong is so shriveled, so shy, and oh! so wee,
It seems to be just worthless, except, perhaps, to pee.

It may go to erection, while you pray in your church;
You're sitting—oh! so proper—when your fly, it gives a lurch.
You're so damned embarrassed, in those sanctified, grim halls,
Seems everyone is watching, while you're shifting your two balls.

It will yearn to philander, when only fit for sleep;
It may dream of gallivanting, when it can hardly creep.
It may fall into torpor, when near the torrid zone,
But howe'er so much a coward, 'tis the only cock you own!

Those Old Red Flannel Drawers

They were tattered, they were torn,
Around the crotch-piece they looked worn,
    Those old red flannel drawers that Maggie wore.
They were hemmed in, they were tucked in,
They were sure the things she fucked in,
    Those old red flannel drawers that Maggie wore.

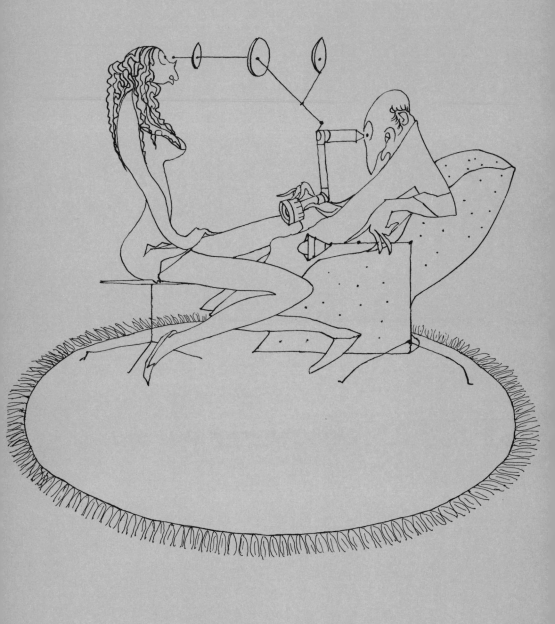

MISCELLANY

Ode to Women over Fifty

They don't tell;
They don't yell;
They don't swell;
And they're grateful as hell!

Evolution

Oh, George, let's not park here

Oh, George, let's not park

Oh, George, let's not

Oh, George, let's

Oh, George

Oh!

The Civil Whore

The Postman came
    On the first of May;
The Policeman came
    The very next day;
Nine months later
    There was hell to pay;
Who fired the shot?
    The Blue or the Gray?

Practical Philosophy

If I take one drink, I can't feel it;

If I take two drinks, I can feel it;

If I take three drinks, anyone can feel it.

So Far

In the parlor a davenport stands,
A couple is sitting there holding hands.
    So far.... no farther!

But now in the parlor a cradle stands;
The mother is weeping and wringing her hands.
    So far.... no father!

The Three Ages of Man

    1.   Tri-weekly

    2.   Try weekly

    3.   Try weakly

Monk to a Nun under Whom He Has Placed a Bible

The holy man is over you;
The holy book is under you;
The holy pole is in your hole,
So wiggle your ass to save your soul.

Mary Meek

Here lie the bones of Mary Meek
Her will was strong, but her won't was weak.

Geographical Estimate of Woman

FROM 14 TO 18:

She is like Africa—partly virgin and partly explored.

FROM 18 TO 24:

She is like Australia—highly developed in the built-up areas.

FROM 24 TO 30:

She is like America—highly technical and always seeking new methods.

FROM 30 TO 40:

She is like Asia—sultry, hot and mysterious.

FROM 40 TO 50:

She is like Europe—somewhat devastated but still interesting in places.

FROM 50 TO 65:

She is like Antarctica—everybody knows where it is but nobody wants to go there.

INDEX TO FIRST LINES

Index to First Lines

Index to First Lines

Index to First Lines

Index to First Lines

Index to First Lines

Index to First Lines

Index to First Lines